APOCALYPSE

THE BOOK FOR OUR TIMES

Rev. Albert Joseph Mary Shamon

CMJ Marian Publishers

Distributors for *Direction for Our Times*
Tan Books and Other Publications

Toll Free 1-888-636-6799
Fax 708-636-2855

www.cmjbooks.com
P.O. Box 661, Oak Lawn, IL 60454

Nihil obstat: Rev. Robert L. Hagedorn
June 14, 1991

Imprimatur: Most Rev. James H. Garland
Auxiliary Bishop of the Archdiocese of Cincinnati
July 3, 1991

The *Nihil obstat* and *Imprimatur* are official declarations that a book or pamphlet is considered to be free from doctrinal or moral error. No implication is contained therein that those who have granted the *Nihil obstat* and *Imprimatur* agree with the contents, opinions, or statements expressed.

Originally published by:
Faith Publishing Company
Milford, OH 45150
1991

Republished in September 1999 by:
The Riehle Foundation
P.O. Box 7
Milford, OH 45150-0007
USA

Library of Congress Catalog Card No: 91-073214

ISBN: 1-880033-00-3

Table of Contents

Publisher's Note

Included in this book are specific references to a number of apparitions of the Blessed Virgin Mary. The publisher recognizes and accepts that the final authority regarding the claimed apparitions at San Nicolas, Argentina, and Medjugorje, Yugoslavia, rests with the Holy See of Rome, to whose judgment we willingly submit.

The apparitions referring to Fatima, Portugal, and to Beauraing and Banneux, Belgium (1932-33) have received the full ecclesiastical approbation.

The Marian Movement of Priests

Throughout this book, the author makes specific references and comparisons to messages alledgedly received by Rev. Stephano Gobbi from the Blessed Virgin Mary contained in the book: TO THE PRIESTS—OUR LADY'S BELOVED SONS. These messages are private revelations to Fr. Gobbi and therefore are not the official teaching of the Catholic Church. The book recording these messages carries the Imprimatur of the Most Reverend James J. Byrne, S.T.D., former Archbishop of Dubuque, on April 4, 1990, which thereby indicates the writing is free of anything contrary to faith or morals.

Interpretation of the Book of Revelation

The publisher acknowledges that comparisons shown herein, as relating to the current world situations, reflect the views of the author and are not meant as a definitive statement on behalf of the Church regarding the Book of Revelation.

v

Outline of this Book:

Background

The title. The Jews in our Lord's day named a book by the first word that began it. Papal encyclicals are named the same way today. The last book of the Bible begins with the words "The revelation of Jesus Christ." The first word "revelation," comes from the Greek word *apocalypsis*. So the last book of the Bible is named *Apocalypse* or *Revelation*.

The *Apocalypse* is a revelation of Jesus Christ to John about what is to happen very soon.

The author. The writer of *Apocalypse* refers to himself as John. Was he John the apostle who wrote the fourth gospel? The early Church Fathers, like Justin and Iraeneus, believed he was; the later Fathers, like Cyprian and John Chrysostom, denied he was.

The John who wrote Apocalypse called himself a prophet, not an apostle. In the *Apocalypse,* the author tells us his name four times; whereas in the fourth gospel, John the apostle never mentions himself by name. In the gospel, the Greek is simple, but correct; in the *Apocalypse* the Greek is rugged, virile and vivid, but incorrect. His Greek is far inferior to that in the gospel; in fact, it is the poorest in the New Testament, written by one who was ill at ease with the language.

It could be, then, that the author of *Apocalypse* was not John the apostle but one of his disciples. He certainly was a Jew, for he thought like one and was steeped in the Old Testament. To distinguish him from John the Apostle, some manuscripts call him John the Divine, that is, the Theologian (Puritans called their theologians "divines"). Some scholars opine that the stylistic differences between the gospel and Revelation are too great to come from the same author. Whether this John is the apostle who wrote the gospel and letters, or one of his disciples is disputed. You can take your pick. Personally, I opt for John the Apostle as the author.

The message. *Apocalypse* is a revelation from Jesus Christ to His persecuted people.

First, the revelation is that an invisible world exists.

Second, this invisible world is revealed as being next door to our visible world, separated if you will by a one-way glass: those in the invisible world can look out to see us, but we can't look in to see them. John suggests this image when he wrote that in front of the throne of God, he saw *something that resembles a sea of glass, like crystal (Rev.* 4:6).

But more important, God, who knows and sees all that is happening here on earth, is deeply concerned about us in our earthly struggle against evil. He knows, He loves, He cares.

Like Him, all the angels and saints in Heaven, also, are on our side; and they help us mightily by their prayers and intercessions.

In other words, we are not alone! In fact the heavenly powers on our side far surpass the evil forces arrayed against us, so that ultimate victory is assured to the good who patiently endure evil.

Third, it is revealed that this God is the Lord of all, even of Caesar. *He is King of kings and Lord of lords (Rev.* 19:16). Therefore, we must not fear. Rather, we must persevere, endure all adversity and persecution with rocklike patience. For in the end, the persecutors will be destroyed; and God and goodness will triumph; and we shall be crowned with eternal glory.

Some Keys to Understanding Apocalypse.

1. Literary Form.

Truth is expressed in a variety of ways. The vehicle an author uses to express truth is called Literary Form.

For instance, if an author wants to entertain, he might use the short story form; if he wants to share news, the letter form; to express deep thought or feeling in figurative language, he will use poetry; to chronicle past events, history; or a life, biography, and so on.

Now in reading anything, it is all-important that we know the Literary Form, else we shall misread what is written. In reading the daily newspaper, we automatically adjust our interpretation according to the Literary Form. For instance, when I'm reading the comics, I know what is written is not for real. When I read the editorial page, I know I am reading opinions. When I read the sports page, I know what I read is fact, and so on.

The Bible is a collection of books, inspired by God. To interpret these books correctly, we must know the Literary Form of each book. To treat the book of *Jonah* as history and not as a parable would be disastrous.

Now the book of *Apocalypse,* or *Revelation,* is a very unique form of literature. It is apocalyptic literature, which has its own stamp and form.

In a Gothic novel or Dracula movie, for instance, we expect dark nights, lightning and ominous thunder rumblings, a black coach pulled by black horses, an eerie castle half in ruins, solitary, situated in a dark forest of half-decayed trees, in which sits a lonely owl, hooting. We rather anticipate all this in that type of novel or movie.

Likewise, apocalyptic literature has its own kind of trappings. It grew out of times of persecution. It was resistance literature, seeking to give hope to the persecuted. So, it was coded, to keep the persecutor in ignorance. Thus apocalypses use numbers, symbols, images drawn from the prophets. The book of *Apocalypse* draws especially from *Ezechiel, Daniel* and *Zechariah.*

If we don't understand this, if we take the symbol for the message, then we will get all kinds of bizarre interpretations of the *Apocalypse.* Hal Lindsay's popular books on *Apocalypse* are often based on literalism rather than on Literary Form. The Chiliasts teach Millenarianism; namely, that Christ will reign on earth for a thousand years with the just before the final judgment. They arrived at this error by taking a text literally (*Rev.* 19:4). The Church condemned this teaching July 21, 1944 (Denzinger, 2296).

2. Numbers.

In the *Apocalypse,* numbers are symbols.

Seven denotes perfection or completeness, because the perfect head should have seven openings.

If seven is the number of perfection, six is the number of imperfection, for imperfection is a lack of something. Thus blindness, a lack of sight, is an imperfection. Since 6 lacks one of 7, it symbolizes imperfection. Six tripled (666) signifies superlative evil. Hence the number of the beast (*Rev.* 13:18).

Half of seven is 3-1/2. Whether it is 3-1/2 days (*Rev.* 11:9; 12:14), or half of a week (seven) of years, which is 42 months or 1,260 days (*Rev.* 11:2-3)—all symbolize a short time and persecution, for the most vicious persecution of the Jews by Antiochus IV lasted 3-1/2 years, June 168 to December 165 B.C. (*Dn.* 7:25; 12:7).

12 is a holy number, it symbolizes the tribes of Israel or the apostles. 4 plus 3 equals 7. 4 times 3 equals 12. 12 squared times 1000 equals 144,000. All these are good numbers. So is 1000: it indicates a vast length of time and connotes triumph.

3. Emperor worship.

At the time *Apocalypse* was written, Caesar worship was the religion of the Empire. Essentially, it meant that the Emperor, because he embodied the spirit of Rome, was divine.

Once a year everyone had to appear before a magistrate, burn a pinch of incense before a statue of Caesar and say, "Caesar is Lord and God." After that, a person could go and practice any other religion he chose. But first, he had to acknowledge the Emperor was God

Basically, this was a ploy used to unite the Roman Empire. You must remember that the Empire of Rome covered 2-1/2 million square miles and included peoples of different races, nations, tongues. To weld this varied mass into a political unity, religion was used. (Charlemagne used religion to forge all Europe into a Holy Roman Empire).

However, none of the religions of the day was universal. But Caesar was. To pledge allegiance to him, as we do to the flag, simply expressed unity with Rome, that one was behind the Emperor. Therefore, to refuse to burn incense before a statue of Caesar and say, "Caesar is Lord and God," was not an act of irreligion, but of treason. Such a person was considered, not an irreligious person, but a bad citizen. That was why Rome was so severe toward those who refused this act of homage.

And yet no Christian could give the title of Lord and God to anyone but Christ. It was the heart of Christianity that Jesus Christ alone is Lord and God!

So the crushing power of the Empire was turned against Christians to annihilate them. This was a new experience, a terrifying experience, for which even the gospels had not prepared them. In this context, the *Apocalypse* was written.

4. The structure of the book.

The Book of Revelation is composed of seven septettes. They are—(1) 7 letters; (2) 7 seals; (3) 7 trumpets; (4) 7 signs; (5) 7 angels; (6) 7 bowls; (7) 7 sights.

Think of a poker player who has seven stacks of chips in front of himself with seven chips in each stack. And he plays them in fours or in threes. In going from one stack to the next, John intersperses visions and scenes.

In using this sevenfold structure, seven times, John brings out the prophetic message of the book. The book of *Revelation* is a prophecy. What does it prophesy?

First, it prophesies to those living in John's day that the wicked are going to be severely punished if they do not repent, and the good will be victorious and richly rewarded if they persevere in witnessing to Jesus.

Second, it prophesies that everything that was happening to the Church and to Christians in the first century will continue to re-occur down through all the centuries till the end of time. In other words, there will always be a huge red dragon around—the devil harassing the Church and her children—and the two beasts (godless governments and false religions) helping the dragon try to destory the Church and her children. There will always be persecution of the good by the evil, with the consequent punishment of the evil, and the eventual triumph of the good. Those are the basic prophecies of the book.

It is also a book of revelation, as well as prophecy. And what is the revelation? It is this: despite the efforts of the dragon and his cohorts, the Lamb and His followers will always triumph. Good will conquer evil. Christ is the One Who was, Who is and Who is to come. In other words, Christ is the One Who is triumphant on every level: in the past, on Calvary; in the present, in the martyrs; and in the future, in the last judgment.

And so the clarion call of John to all the followers of Christ is to "patient endurance." In the words of St. Paul: . . .*all creation is groaning in labor pains even until now; . . . we also groan within ourselves as we wait for adoption, the redemption of our bodies. . . We hope for what we do not see, we wait with endurance (Rom. 8:22-25).*

John plays this theme seven times. The Eastern mind tends to be cyclic rather than linear. Western writers go in a straight line, like driving a car down a highway to a predetermined goal: they have a plot and they develop it point by point to its conclusion. The Eastern writer, on the contrary, pursues a cyclic course. The Hebrews in their Psalms will say something in one line and then repeat it in different words in the very next line. This technique is called "parallelism." John, a Hebrew, used the same device, not once, but seven times. The entire theme is developed in the first septette (the seven letters to the seven churches). Then the same message is retraced again and again (six more times), like climbing a spiral staircase. Or like a merry-go-round, the message comes round and round again and again, but in new, imaginative and creative ways, so that the repetition is not boring but intriguing and joyful.

And since repetition is the heart of understanding, this six-fold repetition helps one grasp the message. Humphrey Bogart's words in *Casablanca*, "Play it again, Sam," apply here. We may not grasp the message of *Revelation* the first time round, so John repeats it for us again and again and again. John takes no chances; he wants his message to get through: the good will always be persecuted, but they will always be victorious; therefore, be patient, wait with endurance.

The Book of Revelation And Today

Visions are an apocalyptic tool. And, of course, they still occur. In our century they seem to be particularly common through the appearances of the Blessed Virgin Mary. Fatima, Banneux and Beauraing, officially sanctioned by the Church, preceded a multitude of claimed appearances which have been happening in the last twenty years.

On May 8, 1972, Don Stefano Gobbi (an Italian priest) began receiving interior locutions from Our Lady with messages specifically for priests, but also for the world. These messages have set forth a spirituality based on the book of Apocalypse and the life of the Church, and have been compiled in a book, "To The Priests, Our Lady's Beloved Sons." I quote from her messages throughout my book to help show that the Apocalypse is truly a book for our times.

Our Lady said to Fr. Stefano Gobbi, *I have wanted to enlighten you concerning the pages of the Apocalypse which refer to the times you are living through. This is to prepare you with me, for the . . . great struggle which is on the point of being fought out between your heavenly Mother and all the forces of evil . . .* (June 17, 1989, #407).
I am the Virgin of Revelation, she says. *I will bring you to the full understanding of Sacred Scripture. Above all, I will read to you the pages of its last book, which you are living . . .* (April 24, 1980, #198).
I am opening for you the sealed book, that the secrets contained in it may be revealed (October 13, 1988, #391).

Our Lady said that this task of opening up the book of the Apocalypse to us was entrusted to her by the Most Holy Trinity (October 13, 1988, #391). *I am being sent by God to open this Book* (Oct. 13, 1987, #366).
Though over the past years, she has given us only fleeting glimpses of parts of the Book, yet during the years 1988-1989, she has focused on it almost exclusively in her locutions to Fr. Gobbi, especially on Chapters 12 and 13.

In Mary's eyes, then, the book of Revelation is most important for us today. A commentary on it is most timely. But to benefit us, Mary's commentary (through her messages to Fr. Gobbi) must also be included.*
Thus we treat Revelation on two levels; on John's level—what it meant in his day; and on Mary's level—what it means in our day.

September 18, 1988, Our Lady said to Fr. Gobbi: *These are ten very important years* [1988-1998]. *These are ten decisive years. I am asking you to spend them with me because you are entering into the final period of the second Advent, which will lead to the triumph of my Immaculate Heart in the glorious coming of my Son Jesus* (#389).

Of course, this does not mean the end of the world, but the end of a world: an era when Satan waxed triumphant. Evil will be crushed, and the Church and the world will experience a sanctity never experienced since Adam and Eve, except, perhaps, in the greatest saints.

There will be a new Heaven and a new earth: the old world, as we know it, where God has been rejected, will be no more. Instead, His Kingdom will come on earth as it is in Heaven— "an eternal and universal kingdom: a kingdom of truth and life; a kingdom of holiness and grace; a kingdom of justice, love and peace" (Preface for the Feast of Christ the King).

Feast of the Immaculate Conception
December 8, 1990

* All references to these locutions will be identified by message number, e.g. #407, #389, #366, etc.

Part I

A. Introduction:
Christ In His Church
(Revelation 1-3)

CHAPTER 1

Introduction
To The Seven Letters

I. **Prologue** (1:1-3)

Like the overture of an opera, the book of *Revelation* begins with a Prologue of three verses.

It starts with the words, *The Revelation of Jesus Christ*. The revelation is from Jesus Christ, not from John. Jesus Christ makes His revelation through an angel to John, who in turn passes it on to the churches, "his servants."

The revelation is about something that is going to happen soon, not at the end of the world or in the twentieth century. It is a revelation of Christ's victory over evil in those first three awful centuries for the Church: through the blood of her martyrs. The final victory came with Constantine the Great (313 A.D.).

And it is a prophecy, foretelling that what is happening in those first centuries will happen again and again in the Church, till the end of time. There will always be (1) persecution of the Church, (2) patient endurance of the good, even martyrdom, and (3) ultimate victory over evil: the blood of martyrs becoming a seed.

The Prologue concludes with the first of seven beatitudes. *Blessed is the one who reads this prophetic message aloud;* apparently, the message is to be read in a liturgical setting by a lector. There is much of the liturgy in *Apocalypse*: hymns and songs of praise by the elders, saints, and angels; then, too, John's vision did occur on the Lord's day (1:10). If the one who reads the message is blessed, equally blessed are those who listen to it and live it.

II. Letters to the Churches of Asia (1:4-8)

John is commanded to write to "the seven churches in Asia." Seven is a symbolic number in Revelation. It denotes perfection, fullness, completeness.

In writing to the seven churches in Asia Minor, John meant his message to be read to all the other churches in the area. The seven churches formed a rough circle, the hub, so to speak, of all the other churches in Asia Minor radiating from them. So the circular letter, an encyclical, as it were, would make the circuit in Asia Minor.

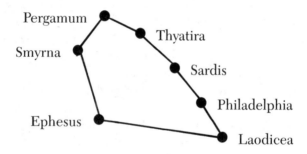

Greeting. Before giving his message, John extends the customary greeting: *Grace to you and peace from him who is and who was and who is to come, and from the seven spirits before his throne, and from Jesus Christ:* that is, grace and peace from God the Father, God the Holy Spirit, and God the Son, Jesus Christ. John then goes on to praise Jesus Christ, saying that all Christians owe Him glory and honor, because "He loved us so much as to redeem us by His blood and make us into a kingdom of priests, giving highest worship to God His Father." This Jesus will come to judge the living and dead, for He is the Alpha (the·first letter of the Greek alphabet) and the Omega (the last letter of the Greek alphabet), that is, both the beginning and the end of all things— everything from A to Z.

III. The First Vision (1:9-20)
Like the prophets, John begins his prophetic message with an inaugural vision. He feels he ought to be listened to, because he practices what he preaches. He endures the troubles and the tribulations which the community suffers. He is in fact exiled to the small barren island of Patmos, precisely because he "proclaimed God's word and gave testimony to Jesus." Patmos is a small island off the coast of Turkey in the Aegean Sea, about 50 miles southeast of Ephesus, used by the Romans as a penal colony.

John does what the Lord is asking all Christians to do, namely, to endure. "Endurance" is a special New Testament word. John will use it repeatedly. It is not just putting up with hardships. Rather, it is a virtue that enables people to remain faithful right through to the bitter end—even through the final days, characterized by terrible distress and affliction for the good.

John was caught up in the spirit on the Lord's Day, a Sunday. Sunday supplanted the Sabbath, because Christ arose from the dead on Sunday. It was a day of worship of the Lord. Hence this vision occurred during a most solemn moment in the Christian week, during a Sunday liturgy.

John heard a voice "as loud as a trumpet." A trumpet was not a musical instrument. It was simply a fanfare introducing a mighty person. The tra-rah-tum-tum of the trumpet simply said: "Ladies and gentlemen, here is God!" The trumpet blowing on Mt. Sinai merely signaled the approach of God to speak or do something important (*Ex.* 19:16-19). The trumpets blown around Jericho caused the walls to come tumbling down

(*Jos.* 6). John is commissioned by the trumpet-voice to write to the seven churches of Asia.[1]

John turned to see who spoke. He has a vision of the Risen Christ, which he describes symbolically, just as the prophets did (*Is.* 6; *Ez.* 1).

He saw *seven gold lampstands.* These are symbols of the seven churches, which are to be lights in the world. *And in the midst of the lampstands one like the son of man.* This is the Risen Christ, the Light of the World, who lives in the midst of the Church and enlightens her.

To describe the Risen Lord, John uses a biblical collage, not to represent a visual image, but to express the divine nature and authority of Jesus.

He wore an ankle length robe, for He is Priest. He has *a gold sash around his chest,* for He is also King (*Ex.*28:4). *The hair of his head was as white as wool or as snow,* for He is all wise (*Dan.* 7:9). *And his eyes were like a fiery flame,* for He is omniscient, sees and knows all things (*Dan.* 10:6). *His feet were like polished brass refined in a furnace,* for He is steadfast, firm and unchangeable (*Ez.* 1:27). *And his voice was like the sound of rushing water,* for like the roar of Niagara, His powerful words drown out the petty articulations of men (*Ez.* 1:24).

In his right hand he held seven stars. Roman emperors were portrayed as holding seven stars in their hands: the seven stars signified the seven planets and thus symbolized the universal dominion of Rome. The Son of Man holds seven stars in his hands as a symbolic challenge to that claim of Rome. Jesus, not the Roman Emperor, has universal domin-

---

1. The problems in the seven churches, as we shall see, were typical of the problems faced by all Christian churches. That is why John's message has universal appeal. And that is why Mary was sent to Fr. Gobbi to enlighten us concerning the pages of the Apocalypse (#407).

ion, "he's got the whole wide world in his hands"; He is *ruler of the kings of the earth (Rev. 1:5).*

A sharp two-edged sword came out of his mouth, symbolizing the word of God that goes right to the heart of things and destroys the wicked (*Heb.* 4:12). *And his face shone like the sun at its brightest,* symbol of the divine majesty (*Mt.* 17:2).

By this collage, John is saying that his message is coming from one who is both God and Man, the Messiah, the Redeemer, the Lord of history and of the Church.

John's reaction to the vision was typical of the Old Testament prophets: "He fell down at his feet as though dead." But Jesus touches him tenderly and calms him with the words: *Do not be afraid.* It was an Old Testament belief that for a sinful human being to see God was to die. Jesus reassures him that He is the author of life, not death. *I hold the keys of death.*

In fact, by the entire vision, the Risen Jesus was saying in effect: "I am priest, king, wise, powerful, steadfast, in complete control, judge and God. I have come, not to create fear, but faith; to strengthen that faith and help My servants endure adversity, even martyrdom. Write that message to the churches. Tell them I stand in their midst to enlighten and to strengthen them. Fear not, then. Be patient. Bear all. Dare all!"

THRACIA

BLACK SEA

AEGEAN SEA

PHRYGIA

PERGAMUM
THYATIRA
SMYRNA • SARDIS
• PHILADELPHIA
EPHESUS • LAODICEA

ISLAND
OF PATMOS

LYCIA

PAMPHYLIA

CRETE

MEDITERRANEAN
SEA

CYPRUS

THE SEVEN CHURCHES
OF ASIA MINOR
TO WHOM JOHN WROTE

CHAPTER 2

The Seven Letters
(the first three)

I. **The format of the letters.**

Each of the seven letters follow the same pattern.

There is an **introduction**: it consists of "to" and "from." Each letter is to a particular church. It is significant that the church addressed is spoken of as IN a particular place; e.g., to the church IN Ephesus, not the church OF Ephesus. (It is inaccurate to speak of an American Church or the Church of Rochester.) Each letter is from the Risen Christ, depicted with one of the characteristics described in the inaugural vision (1:9-16).

The **message** in each letter is twofold: it praises and it blames. Like a good psychologist, John praises "I know"; and then he admonishes "Yet I hold this against you." Two churches are not praised: Sardis and Laodicea; two churches are not warned: Smyrna and Philadelphia.

The first three letters **conclude** with an exhortation and a promise of reward; the last four reverse the pattern: the promise of reward comes first, then the exhortation.

II. **The Seven Churches.**

The churches to which the Letters are written are real historical communities: Ephesus, Smyrna, Pergamum, Thyatira, Sardis, Philadelphia, and Laodicea. The evils condemned are not peculiar to the church addressed—they are present in the Church as a whole. However, the content of the letter

9

is determined generally by some political, historical, geographical or social feature peculiar to the church addressed. For instance, suppose a letter were written to the church in Rochester, New York. Now Rochester is the home of Kodak. The letter might read: "To the angel of the church in Rochester. The one who has eyes like the lens of a camera says this: I know the wonderful picture you have made of the church. Everyone can see the snapshots of the great deeds of your service to the poor and needy.

"But you are still out of focus regarding Catholic education. A wrong attitude is developing. You need more light on this subject. You need to adjust the lenses of your vision. You must see everything in the light of the transmission of the faith. You are too much focused on dollars and cents.

"Now listen. And your reward will be great. You'll have beautiful photos to show God; but no film, no movie, produced by the world's greatest director, will even come close to the show and life God has in store for you for all eternity."

III. To Ephesus (2:1-7)

Ephesus was the greatest port in Asia Minor in the first century and was the crossroads for the East and the West. Cicero called it "the light of Asia." The great temple of Artemis (Diana) there was one of the seven wonders of the world. The sacred prostitution of the temple worship, however, made Ephesus a center of crime and immorality. Also Emperor worship had an early start there. In a word, a more unpromising soil for Christianity could hardly have been imagined.

And yet Paul preached there for two and a half years on his third missionary journey (53-57 A.D.) and made Ephesus one of the great centers of Christianity. Timothy was its first bishop. And John and Mary, the mother of Jesus, dwelt there for a time. The great Council of Ephesus (431 A.D.) defined Mary as the Mother of God (the *theotokos*).

The Letter depicts Christ as in the midst of the church in Ephesus: the One *who walks in the midst of the seven gold lampstands.* He commends the Ephesians for resisting false teachings; for doing good works; and for enduring trials and persecution patiently. But they have lost the love they had at first. Deep concern about orthodoxy has made them legalistic, so much so that they have forgotten what it means to love one another. Christ says: "Hate false teaching, but don't hate one another."

Then Christ points out to them the three steps to conversion: realization, repentance, and action. Those were the steps taken by the prodigal son: first, coming to his senses; then "I have sinned"; and he got up and went back to his father (*Lk.* 15:17-20). So Christ says: "Realize how far you have fallen. Repent. Do the works you used to do. If you persevere, you will regain the paradise lost."

IV. **To Smyrna** (2:8-11)

Smyrna, 30 miles north of Ephesus, was one of the loveliest cities of Asia Minor. It was a great trading center, enjoying a land-locked harbor. Behind the city rose hills crowned with noble buildings and temples. Through the city ran a golden street, like a golden necklace at the foot of the hills, crowned with buildings. In 600 B.C., Smyrna died, was destroyed by the Lydians; but in 200 B.C., it came to life again, was rebuilt.

Besides its beauty, Smyrna was noted for its unwavering loyalty to Rome and its fine arts. In fact, Smyrna was one of the seven cities that claimed to being the birthplace of Homer.

The Jewish community there was both large and most influential. Christ refers to them as false Jews, *the assembly of Satan.* They were responsible for the persecution of the Christians. Christ urges the Christians to be faithful during these trials, for they will last only for a short while ("ten days"). The most famous martyr was the Bishop of Smyrna, St. Polycarp, disciple of St. John, and faithful to God even unto death by fire (155 A.D.).

The Lord Jesus, Who, like Smyrna, had died and had risen, has nothing but praise for the church in Smyrna. He knows the slander of the so-called Jews, the assembly of Satan. As Smyrna was so loyal to Rome, the risen Lord urges the Christians to be faithful throughout the short persecutions. And like Smyrna, they too will be crowned, not with buildings, but with eternal life. The second death, hell, will never touch them.

V. To Pergamum (2:12-17)

Pergamum was about 44 miles northeast of Smyrna. It was called the city "where Satan's throne is," because it was the center of Emperor worship in Asia.

Rome saw in the deification of the Emperor, a much needed way to unify its vast empire. It was a law that once a year every Roman citizen had to go to the temple of the Emperor, burn a pinch of incense to the divinity of Caesar, and say, "Caesar is Lord." Of course no Christian could do that; for the Christian, "Jesus is Lord." The Romans could not understand this opposition and so regarded Christians as revolutionaries, disloyal to the State.

Also, at Pergamum, the proconsul had the *jus gladii*, the right of the sword, which meant he could put a man to death on the spot, just on his say-so. Thus a sword always hung over the head of the Christians at Pergamum. At any time someone could denounce them and jeopardize their lives. The Letter reminds Christians to stand firm, because the One who has the real sharp, two-edged sword is not the proconsul, but the risen Christ.

Pergamum was famous too for its library. The word "parchment" is derived from Pergamum. In the third century B.C., the King of Pergamum tried to bribe the librarian, Aristophanes, away from the great library at Alexandria. When King Ptolemy of Egypt discovered this, he imprisoned Aristophanes and boycotted sending all papyrus ("paper") to Pergamum. To beat the boycott, the scholars of Pergamum took the skins of animals and rubbed them smooth for writing. These skins were called *Pergamene charta*, sheets from Pergamum or parchment *(per-char-mene)*.

Christ says to the Christians of Pergamum, "I know you live where Satan's throne is and still you have not denied your faith. But there is danger that you are beginning to cut corners. Some of you are listening to the teachings of Balaam and the Nicolaitans."

The Nicolaitans were like Balaam. Balaam *(Num.* 25:1-3) compromised the Hebrews coming out of Egypt by getting them to intermarry with Moabite women and then accept the worship of the Baals, which most always involved immorality.

Heathens had no idea of chastity. Relations before marriage and outside of marriage were considered normal: "doing what comes naturally." The Nicolaitans opined, "Must a Christian be so different? What harm to go along to get along?"

Also, heathens had no hesitation in eating foods offered to idols. All business banquets and social festivities had meats offered to idols. "Why," taught the Nicolaitans, "should Christians absent themselves and thus suffer grievous economic losses? After all, religion is in the soul, not in the body. The body cannot sully the soul; the soul is the important thing. Therefore, love God and forget about what the body does."

St. Paul had to contend with this error with the Galatians. *You were called for freedom...but do not use this freedom as an opportunity for the flesh (Gal.* 5:13).

The Nicolaitans sought to persuade Christians that there was nothing wrong with a prudent conformity to the world's standards. Instead of raising the world up to the standards of Christianity, they were bringing Christianity down to the standards of the world.

The risen Christ said He would make war against these teachers. His anger would be directed, not against the church, but against those misleading and seducing the church. For the straying, He has pity; for those leading astray, He has hottest wrath.

To those who are victorious, the risen Christ promises the hidden manna and a white amulet with a new name on it. The hidden manna is the bread of life given to those who resist the temptation to dine at heathen banquets where the meat had been sacrificed to idols. A white amulet with a new name on it was like our sacramentals, far different from the charms pagans used to protect themselves from evil. The pagan charms were useless against evil; whereas the Christian sacramental has with it the power of God.

Remember our poker player? The seven Letters constitute his first stack of chips. He plays this stack in three and then in four.

In the Letter to Ephesus, there are the words: *You have tested those who call themselves apostles.* In the Letter to Smyrna, the words: *Those who claim to be Jews and are not.* In the Letter to Pergamum, the words: *The teaching of the Nicolaitans.* False apostles, false Jews, false prophets.

St. Paul in his farewell address at Miletus, to the Ephesian clergy, said: *Keep watch over yourselves and over the whole flock of which the Holy Spirit has appointed you overseers,...* *I know that after my departure savage wolves will come among you, and they will not spare the flock. And from your own group, men will come forward perverting the truth to draw the disciples away after them. So be vigilant...* (Acts 20:28-31).

More than once the New Testament insists on the necessity of testing. *Test the spirits to see whether they belong to God, because many false prophets have gone out into the world.* (1 Jn. 4:1). Again to the Thessalonians, Paul says, *Test everything* (1 Thess. 5:21). He insists that when prophets speak that they be tested by other prophets (1 Cor. 14:29). A person cannot palm off his own private views as gospel or compromise it, as the Nicolaitans and Jezebel were trying to do.

To sift truth from error, Jesus demanded this test: *By their fruits you will know them* (Mt. 7:16). The only trouble with this rule is that sometimes we find out only after the damage has been done.

To complement this rule, therefore, another good rule is this: Does what is being taught square with the authoritative teaching of the Catholic Church on faith and morals? For instance, the Council of Jerusalem (50 A.D.) ordered pagan converts *to abstain from meat sacrificed to idols. . .and from unlawful marriage* (*Acts* 15:28-29). The so-called apostles, the so-called Jews, and the so-called teachers (the Nicolaitans, Jezebel) rejected the Council's teachings. For the Christian, that fact is warning enough that here one has wolves in sheep's clothing.

CHAPTER 3

THE SEVEN LETTERS
(the last four)

I. **To Thyatira** (2:18-29)

Thyatira is about forty miles southeast of Pergamum. It was on the road connecting Pergamum and Sardis. Much traffic passed through the town. Its chief industry was dyeing and its main trade was in woolen goods. Lydia, Paul's first convert in the West, was from Thyatira and dealt in purple fabric in Philippi (*Acts* 16:14).

Thyatira had many trade guilds. Guilds of workers in wool, leather, linen, and bronze; guilds of dyers and potters, and so on. And here is where problems arose for the Christians. To refuse to belong to a guild was commercial suicide.

Yet Christians had to refuse. Why? Because guilds often had banquets for their patron god or goddess. These banquets were in a temple; or, if elsewhere, they always began and ended with sacrifices to the gods and served meats that had been offered to idols. These banquets generally degenerated into drunken orgies and immorality.

The problem came when certain persons in the Church felt that business is business. A woman named Jezebel taught, "Why not join the guilds for business purposes? What harm is there in sharing their ceremonies and festivities? All we are concerned with is the almighty dollar." It would be like a Catholic today reasoning, "Why shouldn't I join the Masons, embrace their religion, for as a Mason I can make important business contacts?"

16

Even though Thyatira is the least important of the seven cities, yet the letter written to her is the longest. Perhaps this is so, because the evil of compromise with the world is an evil threatening all the churches. The Letter opens with praise, as usual. *I know your love, faith, service, and endurance.* But then the One whose eyes flamed like fire in blazing wrath and in penetrating into the very hearts and minds of men upbraids the church, because *you tolerate the woman Jezebel.*

Who this Jezebel is we really do not know. Perhaps she was a clone of Jezebel of old (*1 Kgs.* 16:31). Jezebel of old seduced King Ahab, and Israel, from the worship of the true God. The new Jezebel was doing the same to Christianity. She did not want to destroy it, only to modify it to conform to the world. Perhaps she is a symbol of all who feel that if the Church's standards clashed with business, then the Church's standards must yield. After all, one must make a living.

Those who followed her teachings (*committed adultery with her*) would be punished; those who embraced her teachings (*her children*) would be exterminated.

No doubt those who followed her teachings and compromised with the world for business sake prospered and were probably lavish in giving to the church. No doubt those who attended the trade guilds gave generously to appeals for the poor. They looked like real Christians. No doubt even Jezebel must have presented a fine picture. She certainly could speak, for she was a prophetess. But the risen Christ, with eyes like a fiery flame, can pierce the outward show, search the mind and heart and give to each what his works deserve.

But to the others not seduced by Jezebel, the Risen Lord says, "Hold fast to what you have until I come." And He promises that they will share in the missionary conquests of the Messiah; and, in the resurrection victory over death, they will shine like the morning star.

II. To Sardis (3:1-6)

Sardis is about thirty miles south southeast of Thyatira. Once it was the capital of Lydia. The River Pactolus, which flowed through the town, provided it with so much gold that the wealth of its king, Croesus, 600 B.C., became proverbial. Even today we say, "As rich as Croesus."

The city sat on a plateau on the side of Mt. Tmolus. Fifteen hundred feet up in the air, it was deemed impregnable. So smug were the Sardians with their riches and so complacent about the strength of their city, that they left it unguarded. As a result, twice in its history Sardis was taken by surprise: first by Cyrus in 546 B.C. and then by Antiochus in 195 B.C. Hence the admonition, "Be watchful."

At the time John wrote, Sardis was known for two things: its dyeing and woolen industries and its profligacy. The church in Sardis seems to have reflected the history of the city: once its spiritual life was rich, but now it was bankrupt.

The Risen Lord has seven spirits and seven stars. The church at Sardis (one of the seven stars) needs new life, the sevenfold gifts of the Spirit. The Church there may look alive, but it is really dead. In fact it is so dead that there is no need to persecute her, to waste shot and shell on her. A living church pricks the consciences of men and draws opposition; when no one even notices her, it is dead. *Woe to you,* said Jesus, *when all speak well of you (Lk.* 6:26). That was the condition of the church in Sardis.

If anything was to be salvaged in the church, the Christians must wake up. They are not so good as they think. They must rouse themselves from their smugness and complacency. "Be watchful!"

In His agony, Jesus said to His apostles, *Watch and pray that you may not undergo the test (Mt.* 26:4). As eternal vigilance is the price of safety for drivers, so eternal watchfulness is the price of salvation for Christians. If they are not watchful, what happened twice to Sardis could happen to them. They could be taken by surprise, for the Risen Lord will come like a thief in the night. "The gods," so goes an old Latin saying, "walk on feet that are wrapped with wool." But the Christian who is always watchful will never be caught unawares.

A teacher once told his students that the surest way to be saved was to live the last day of their life for God. "But," the students protested, "we don't know when that day is." "Then," answered the teacher, "live today for the Lord, it may be your last day." "If you are not watchful," says Jesus, "I will come like a thief and catch you unawares." Twice in history, Sardis was caught off guard to her deep regret. Jesus warns her not to let the same thing happen again, spiritually. It won't if they remember their first fervor and enthusiasm that followed upon the preaching of the gospel; if they keep the teachings of the gospel; and finally, if they repent and snap out of their apathy. They must stop drifting, stop procrastinating. They must decide for God!

The faithful few will be dressed in the joyful white garment of purity and victory. And their names will be written in the book of life.

III. To Philadelphia (3:7-13)

Philadelphia was about 28 miles southeast of Sardis. It was a border town, founded about 140 B.C. to open the door for Greek culture to the East. Attalus built it. Because of his great love for his brother Eumenes, Attalus was nicknamed Philadelphos, and the city was named after him.

Philadelphia was a city of earthquakes. The quakes not only came, but they often continued on for years. Little tremors were an almost daily occurrence, so most of the population lived in tents away from the city buildings, lest the falling stones kill them. Then, too, to receive "a new name" struck a responsive chord in them, because twice Philadelphia had changed its name in gratitude to the Caesars for the help given them after earthquakes.

In the introduction to the Letter, the Risen Christ is called *the holy one, the true, who holds the key of David.* He is holy, because He shares the life of God. He is true, because He is for real, the truth. And He holds the key of David, for He alone can open the door to the Kingdom of Heaven for those who receive the gospel. Among these one day will be the Jews themselves, the inveterate enemies of Christians. So the Christians are to be a door for the gospel. Even to this day, Philadelphia is the one Christian city in the Turkish empire with a resident Bishop, five churches, and thousands of Christians.

Like Smyrna, Philadelphia receives no reproach. Instead only a promise. If they remain loyal, and follow the example of Christ's patient endurance, they will see at least the beginnings of the triumph of Christ, and in any testing they will be kept safe by Christ. In the end they will belong to God and to Christ in glory in the new Jerusalem.

IV. To Laodicea (3:14-22)

Laodicea was about 40 miles south of Philadelphia. It was built by Antiochus II (261-244 B.C.) and named after his wife Laodice.

Three facts about the city throw light on the Letter: it was a banking center and extremely wealthy; it manufactured clothing and woolen carpets; it had a medicine school, famous for its ointments for eyes and ears.

The Letter begins with a strange title: *The Amen.* The Risen Christ is the great Amen—the perfect witness of the things of God to mankind. He has absolutely nothing good to say about the church in Laodicea. Almost 30 years before, St. Paul found it necessary to issue this warning to the Bishop of Laodicea, *Tell Archippus, "See that you fulfill the ministry that you received in the Lord."* (Col. 4:17).

Because the Laodiceans are neither cold nor hot, they are nauseating. Right near Laodicea are the hot mineral springs of Hieropolis. The taste of these waters, as well as the smell, induced nausea. So did the indifference or lukewarmness of the Laodiceans to the Risen Christ. A cold drink or a hot drink is potable; but a tepid one is not.

In fact, Christ condemned indifference unsparingly. A great obstacle to Christianity is neutrality. You cannot drive your car in neutral. Likewise, Christ can do nothing with one who doesn't care. Better the fierce opposition of his enemies than the unconcern of His friends. Studdert-Kennedy in his poem, *Indifference,* has expressed how revolting to Christ is indifference:

> When Jesus came to Golgotha, they hanged Him
>   on a tree,
> They drove great nails through hands and feet,
>   and made a Calvary;
> They crowned Him with a crown of thorns,
>   red were His wounds and deep,
> For those were crude and cruel days, the human
>   flesh was cheap.
>
> When Jesus came to Birmingham, they simply
>   passed Him by,
> They never hurt a hair of Him, they only let Him die;
> For men had grown more tender, and they would
>   not give Him pain,
> They only just passed down the street, and left
>   Him in the rain.
>
> Still Jesus cried, "Forgive them,
>   for they know not what they do,"
> And still it rained the winter rain
>   that drenched Him through and through;
> The crowds went home and left the streets without a
>   soul to see,
> And Jesus crouched against a wall and cried for
>   Calvary.

Perhaps the Laodiceans got that way because their great wealth made them feel no need for God; because the fine garments they produced hid the shame of their spiritual nakedness; because their eye ointments, the best in the world, crowded out the thought that they could ever be spiritually blind.

So the Risen Christ exhorts Christians there to buy gold tried by the fire, to have a faith tested by life, so that they would become truly rich—able to meet any of life's situations; to cover up their spiritual nakedness by putting on the white garment of a good life; and to smear their eyes with ointment so that they might see themselves as they truly are.

Then the Risen Christ utters one of the most famous lines in Scripture: *Those whom I love, I reprove and chastise.* God's reproof is not a severe scolding, nor a violent accusation, but rather a reproof much like that of Nathan to David after his terrible sins of adultery and murder. Nathan's reproof opened up David's eyes. God reproves, not to punish, but to convert. And he chastises as the father does his child to have it end up well. It is the crushed grape that gives the wine. It is the disciplined athlete that wins the crown.

So the Risen Christ stands at the door and knocks. What a grace! He comes; He seeks us, not the other way round. The door is the human heart, and we are free. Just as we never would go into a house unless invited, so Jesus never enters a heart unless invited (*Lk.* 24:28). He goes as far as He can: He comes, He stands, He knocks, and He waits for our response. Love can go no further.

What an opportunity! If one opens the door, then Christ comes in, not just for a chat or a hurried call, but for dinner—for only by eating together with Him can we build up a friendship with Him. Dining with Him here (by prayer and the Eucharist) guarantees a place for us at the eternal banquet of Heaven.

CHAPTER 4

The Prophecies in the Seven Letters

Remember, the book of *Revelation* is a prophetic book in the sense that what has happened in the Church and to the Church in John's time, will continue to happen in and to the Church till the end of time.

Thus the Church in our century is plagued with the same four problems that beset the Church in John's day: 1. **lukewarmness**, 2. **slanderous attacks**, 3. **false teaching**, and 4. **complacency**.

1. Perhaps the biggest trial for the Church in any age is the indifference and lukewarmness of its members. That is probably why the letters to the Church in Ephesus and Laodicea were put first and last. It was probably because of the importance of the warning given in both letters about the dangers of lukewarmness and indifference. These maladies afflict the Church today.

Around 1937, Jesus requested Sister Maria H. Faustina Kowalska to write down a novena prayer to the Divine Mercy, which was to begin on Good Friday and end on the first Saturday after Easter. *I desire,* said Jesus, *that during these nine days, you bring souls to the fount of My mercy...On each day you will bring to my Heart a different group of souls.* When Sister said, "I do not know which souls to bring first to your Most Compassionate Heart," Jesus replied that He would tell her.

23

On the ninth day of the Novena, Jesus said, *Bring to me souls that are lukewarm . . . These souls wound my heart most painfully. My soul suffered the most dreadful loathing in the Garden of Olives because of lukewarm souls. They were the reason why I cried out: 'Father, take this cup away from Me, if it be Your will.' For them the last hope of salvation is to flee to My mercy.*

Jesus described lukewarm souls to Sister Faustina like this: *Souls without love and without devotion, souls full of egoism and self-love, souls full of pride and arrogance, souls full of deceit and hypocrisy, lukewarm souls who have just enough warmth to keep them alive: My heart cannot bear this. All the graces that I pour out upon them flow off them as off the face of a rock.* (Diary, VI, 73-74).

"An author," William Barclay said, "can write a good biography if he loves his subject, or if he hates his subject, but not if he is coldly. . .indifferent to his subject" (On *Rv.* 1, p. 179). If a person feels intensely about something one way or the other, you are able to do something with him; but if he doesn't feel at all, then it is almost impossible to do anything with him. That is why the Risen Christ vehemently condemns indifference or lukewarmness.

2. The second great trial of the Church today, and in almost every age, is bigotry or slanderous attacks. The Church in Smyrna and Philadelpia suffered from slander by Satan's assembly, those who falsely called themselves Jews.

Congressman Robert K. Dornan of California said in the House of Congress: "Believe it or not, Mr. Speaker, there is no group in America that suffers more open or blatant discrimination than Roman Catholicism.

"Not black Americans, not African-Americans, not Jewish Americans, not Hispanic Americans, no one, not any group or person suffers the bigotry that my Church does today. . ." (Congressional Record, Oct. 19, 1990, H.10684).

Today the Catholic Church is targeted by the godless media

and godless groups, as never before in American history. Under the shibboleth of Separation of Church and State, prayer has been outlawed in schools, pornography has been let loose on society, abortion legitimized. So vicious is the attack on the moral values of Christianity that secularistic judges have been imposing unjust sentences on pro-life advocates. What an indictment of anti-Christian bigotry is expressed in the couplet: "Be a hero, save a whale. Save a baby and go to jail!"

3. The third great threat to the Church that recurs again and again is that which comes from false prophets.

One of the ploys of the false prophet is to urge compromise with the world. Here is what the Mother of God said to Fr. Gobbi: *You are now living in obscure times, because in all kinds of ways an attempt is being made to reach a compromise between God and Satan; between good and evil; between the spirit of Jesus and the spirit of the world... Like a cloud of invisible poisonous gas, a spirit which jumbles the things of God with those of the world is expanding and succeeding in depriving the Word of God of its vigor, and in despoiling the announcement of the Gospel of its force!* (#254). In Pergamum and Thyatira, the false teachings of the Nicolaitans and Jezebel advised compromise with the world.

The other false prophets are the so-called theologians who publicly dissent with the Magisterium of the Church. Their philosophy is anti-papal, anti-hierarchy, anti-dogma, and, if pro-anything, they endorse a very wishy-washy moral code.

Our Lady said to Fr. Gobbi: *...how deeply the scandal, even of bishops who do not obey the Vicar of my Son and who sweep a great number of my poor children along the path of error, wounds and pains my heart.* (#106).

Besides this open rebellion against the Pope, Our Lady said, *there is also another way, more subtle and dangerous. It is that of proclaiming one's unity openly, but of dissenting from him interiorly, letting his teaching fall into a void and, in prac-*

tice, doing the contrary of what he says (#170). This is like the eleventh station of the cross, because it immobilizes the Church, nails it down.

4. The last great threat to the Church now and always is complacency. This was the problem that afflicted the Church in Sardis. In America this evil goes by the name of Secular Humanism. Secular means the world; and Humanism means man. Secular Humanism is the new religion in America: it says this world is everything and man is its god. It claims that God, Himself, has no room in this world nor in mankind's life.

Thus Our Lady lamented to Fr. Gobbi that these are the times when a civilization without God is being constructed, and all humanity is being led to live without Him (#409).

How does one get this way? The same way Sardis got that way—its riches. Affluence, technological advances, a superfluity of this world's goods can lure one into believing he or she does not need God. I think that is what we mean when we pray, "Lead us not into temptation"—the temptation of thinking we don't need God; the temptation that we can make it on our own; the temptation to depend totally on one's own resources.

Yet how limited are the powers of money. Money may be able to buy a bed, but not sleep; books, but not brains; food, but not an appetite; clothes, but not beauty; a house, but not a home; medicine, but not health; amusement, but not happiness; a crucifix, but not salvation.

God warned the Sardians, "Watch, wake up." Put a frog into boiling water and it will hop right out. But put the frog in cold water, then heat it .0036 of a degree fahrenheit per second and at the end of two and one half hours the frog will be found dead. The explanation is that the water is heated so gradually that the frog never becomes aware of the rising temperature and is boiled to death without a struggle.

Is not the danger here in America that of being lulled into a false confidence by our affluence? Ought we not watch? Wake up!

Every one of the seven Letters finishes with the words: *Whoever has ears ought to hear what the Spirit says to the Churches.* This sentence tells us two things.

First, it tells us that the messages of these Letters are for everyone. The Risen Christ is speaking to "whoever has ears." We all have ears. So the Risen Christ is saying to each of us, "I mean you! All of you who have ears to hear what the Spirit says."

Secondly, the Risen Christ is saying that the messages of these Letters are not just to the seven churches in Asia Minor, but "to the churches" down through the centuries.

The Letters have local color, it is true, but the messages are universal. Christ is speaking to the Church of yesterday, today and tomorrow, for He—the One Who was, Who is and Who is to come—stands forever among the seven golden lampstands: the Church!

*"Behold, I stand at the door and knock. If anyone hears my voice
and opens the door, [then] I will enter his house and dine with him,
and he with me."*   Rev. 3:20

Part I

B. The Church Suffering
(*Revelation* 4-9)

CHAPTER 5

The Second Vision
(*Revelation* 4-5)

The first vision (*Rev.* 1:9-20), introducing the seven letters
to the seven churches in Asia Minor, was a vision of the Risen
Christ standing here on earth in the midst of the seven
lampstands—a vision of Christ in His Church.

The second vision (*Rev.* 4-5) is a vision of the Trinity. God
the Father is seated on a throne, surrounded by twenty-four
elders and four living creatures, with a scroll in His right
hand. God the Holy Spirit flashes forth from the One on the
throne, like lightning, thunder and seven flaming torches. God
the Son is seen as a Lamb, standing, though He seemed to
have been slain.

The first vision showed the Risen Christ in relation to His
Church. This second vision shows the Risen Christ in relation to God the Father in Heaven and to the Church in world
history. The scroll in the right hand of the One Who sits
on the throne is God's plan for the history of the world:
the mystery hidden from ages (*Col.* 1:26), namely to save all
people through the death and resurrection of the Lamb
(*Eph.* 1:9-10).

Visions were important to apocalyptic writers, for these gave
them authority to speak God's word to His people. The mis-
sions of the prophets always began with an inaugural vision.
That is what gave them the authority to speak. They were
the mouthpieces of God. In our time, the six seers of Med-

31

jugorje (like the seers of Lourdes, Fatima, etc.) are listened to by millions precisely because they claim to have visions from Our Lady.[2]

A vision is seeing. The first part of the vision of God the Father begins with John seeing an open door. The Jews thought that the heavens was a solid vault entered by an actual trapdoor (*Ps.* 24:7).

A vision, too, is hearing. John hears the Risen Christ inviting him, with a trumpetlike voice, to enter Heaven through the open door. "Come up here and I will show you what must happen in time to come" (the purpose of the vision).

Up there, John sees God the Father. Jews never mention the name of God; hence John speaks of Him as *One seated on the throne.* He is seated on a throne, for He is the King of the entire world. As the song puts it: "He's got the whole wide world in His hands," not Caesar.

John, like any other Jew, rigorously shunned trying to describe God in anthropomorphic terms. Instead, he resorted to the standard description of God, namely, in terms of light—a light of dazzling beauty, like precious gems. Thus the One seated on the throne sparkled like jasper (a diamondlike rock), and carnelian (blood-red stone); and around His throne was a halo as brilliant as green emerald.

Surrounding the throne were twenty-four elders, representing the people of God, who are the descendants of the twelve tribes of Israel and the twelve apostles. They were dressed in white garments with gold crowns on their heads—for God's people are a priestly people and a kingly people.

From the throne came flashes of lightning, rumblings and peals of thunder, signifying God's acting or intervening in the world (*Ex.* 19:16; *Ez.* 21:13). He acts through His Holy Spirit:

---

2. On June 24, 1981, Our Lady has allegedly appeared in Medjugorje, Yugoslavia to six children. These apparitions have been going on daily for the last 10 years. The Church is investigating these apparitions. At present she has neither approved nor condemned them.

the seven flaming torches burning in front of the throne. The
floor in front of the throne was like a sea of glass that was
crystal-clear. Although the world is far distant from God, God's
vision of the world is not hindered, for glass is transparent.
"All things are open and naked to his eyes."

In the center and around the throne were four living creatures with eyes in front and back. They symbolize the four
corners of the earth and the four seasons, as well as the four
faces of Christ seen through the evangelists—all of which
glorify and praise God.

One of the four resembled a lion; the second, a calf; the
third, a human being; and the fourth, an eagle. The lion, king
of wild beasts; the calf (ox), king of domestic beasts; a human
being, king of all creation; and the majestic eagle, swiftest
of birds—all reveal by symbol how much more noble, stronger,
wiser, swifter, must be the Creator of all creatures! God is
King of kings: Lord of all creation—regal, strong, wise, swift
to help; with eyes, front and back, that see into the past and
look into the future.

The four living creatures had six wings, for God is swift
to act in behalf of His people; and His people include all
the descendants of the 12 tribes and the 12 apostles, for
$6 \times 4 = 24$. They were covered with eyes inside and out, to
make sure that nothing in the world escapes God.

Since all creation is subject to God the Father, it declares
His glory day and night (*Ps.* 19:1). First, God's holiness is
praised. God is thrice holy: holy, because all things he has
made are good; holy, because all things work together unto
our good; holy, because He loves good, always. Secondly, God
is proclaimed as the Lord God Almighty, not Caesar. For God,
not Caesar, is forever, eternal: the One Who was, Who is,
and Who is to come.

Each time God intervenes in the world in behalf of His
own, the twenty-four elders, the representatives in Heaven
of God's people, worship the Father by throwing down their
crowns before the throne exclaiming that the Father is *Domi-*

nus et Deus, Lord and God, not Caesar; and that He alone
is worthy of glory, honor and praise, because He alone is the
Creator of everything that is made.

What is the message of this chapter?
Remember the hallmark of apocalyptic literature is Con-
ceptual Symbolism; that is, using symbols to express an idea.
The important thing is the idea, not the image used to express
it. The message is more important than the medium.

Here, John speaks with authority, like the prophets; because,
like them, he has had a vision of God and has heard a message from Him.

Secondly, this message comes from One Who is King of
kings (seated on a throne, with 24 elders taking off their crowns
before Him); Who rules the world (four living creatures), in
wisdom (eyes inside and out), Who is swift in governing it
(6 wings); Who is indescribably beautiful, scintillating and
sparkling like precious gems; Who loves good and hates evil—
for He is thrice holy; Who is Lord God, not Caesar, for He
alone is Creator of all creation.

Therefore, harrassed Christians must not fear Caesar, for
He is not Lord; rather, they should take heart for their Lord
is true God, almighty, all-seeing, all-wise, swift to help and
defend His own.

In the vision of Chapter 4, John portrayed God the Father
as holy, creator, all-powerful and all-wise ruler of the universe. He saw the Commander-in-chief with all His forces:
the Holy Spirit with His seven gifts.

In Chapter 5, John reveals the Commander's Chief of Oper-
ations: the Lamb of God.
The Commander's plan of action against the powers of evil
in the world is written on a scroll, with writing on both sides,
for His plan encompasses all the world; and with seven seals,
for His plan is for all ages. In his letter to the Ephesians,
Paul unfolded this plan, namely, to restore all things in Christ.

When no one in Heaven, on earth, or under the earth was able to open the scroll and break its seals, John wept bitterly. For he wanted to offer some consolation to the Christians suffering for their faith. He wanted to reveal to them God's plan and purpose for all—the direction of history, and in this way give suffering Christians a powerful motivation to endure all patiently. He wanted to show that patient endurance makes sense, not nonsense. Everything that is happening had been planned by God and so will work to good.

One of the elders said to John: *Do not weep. The Lion of Judah, the root of David, has won the right to open the scroll.* "Lion," because Jesus conquered death; and "root," for He was born of David's line when this once glorious tree had been cut down to its roots, to almost nothingness, to a Joseph and Mary, just "ordinary" people.

This lion was a Lamb, that seemed to have been slain, bearing the marks of His passion; yet standing, for He was risen from the dead. He stood between the throne and the elders, for He is the mediator between God and His people. He had seven horns; therefore, all powerful. He had seven eyes; therefore, all-knowing. He had the seven spirits of God; therefore, the Holy Spirit and His sevenfold gifts. And this Spirit, given Him by the Father, He sent out into the whole world.

This lamb took the scroll and opened it, for He is the Word of God Who has made known to us God's plan for all mankind.

Because the Word-made-flesh came to reveal the Father's plan and love for us, all the heavens reverberate in a hymn of praise, that ripples out to the angels, and finally to all creatures in Heaven, on earth and under the earth.

First, the four living creatures and the twenty-four elders adore the Lamb—John's affirmation of the Divinity of Christ. The elders with harps (offering songs of praise) and golden bowls of incense (offering the prayers of the faithful on earth), declare that the Lamb is worthy to open the scroll. For by

His bloody death, He has won for His Father in Heaven a kingly people and a priestly people from all nations.

Then countless angels (literally, one hundred million plus one million) affirm what the elders had said and in thunderous voices cry out that the Lamb slain is worthy to receive honor and glory and blessing.

Finally, all creation, in response to the angels' declaration, praises the One on the throne and the Lamb. Like a mighty chorus in Handel's "Messiah," they cry out, "Here's to you both, blessing and honor, glory and might, forever and ever." To all this, the four living creatures add "Amen"; and the elders fall down and worship.

CHAPTER 6

In Our Own Day
A Replay of the Second Vision

After the vision of Hell, given to the seers of Fatima on July 13, 1917, Our Lady promised that she would come again to ask for the consecration of Russia to her Immaculate Heart in order to convert Russia.[3]

Mary fulfilled that promise on June 13, 1929, to Lucia, then a Dorothean nun in the convent at Tuy, in northern Spain. Here is Sister Lucia's account of that vision.

"I had sought and obtained permission from my superiors and confessor to make a Holy Hour from eleven o'clock until midnight, every Thursday to Friday night. Being alone one night, I knelt near the altar rails in the middle of the chapel and, prostrate, I prayed the prayers of the Angel."

One of these prayers is to the most Holy Trinity:

3. Fatima is a small village in the very center of Portugal, about 70 miles north of Lisbon. Beginning on May 13, 1917, Our Lady appeared six times (on the 13th of each month) to three Fatima children, Lucia Santos (aged 10), and her two cousins, Francisco (aged 9) and Jacinta Marto (aged 7). On October 13, she peformed the miracle of the sun.
   Before these apparitions began, an angel taught the children prayers and prepared them for Our Lady's visits.
   In 1930, the Church approved of these apparitions.

37

"O most Holy Trinity, Father, Son and Holy Spirit,
I adore Thee profoundly. I offer Thee the most precious Body, Blood, Soul and Divinity of Jesus
Christ, . . . in reparation for the outrages, sacrileges
and indifference by which He is offended.

"By the infinite merits of the Sacred Heart of
Jesus, and the Immaculate Heart of Mary, I beg
the conversion of poor sinners."

The vision Sr. Lucia received was, we might say, a graphic
visualization of the above Trinitarian prayer.

"Feeling tired, I then stood up and continued
to say the prayers with my arms in the form of a
cross. The only light was that of the sanctuary lamp.

"Suddenly the whole chapel was illumined by
a supernatural light, and above the altar appeared
a cross of light, reaching to the ceiling. In a brighter
light on the upper part of the cross, could be seen
the face of a man and his body as far as the waist;
upon his breast was a dove of light; nailed to the
cross was the body of another man. A little below
the waist, I could see a chalice and a large host
suspended in the air, on to which drops of blood
were falling from the face of Jesus Crucified and
from the wound in His side. These drops ran down
on to the host and fell into the chalice.

"Beneath the right arm of the cross was Our Lady
and in her hand was her Immaculate Heart. (It was
Our Lady of Fatima, with her Immaculate Heart
in her left hand, without sword or roses, but with
a crown of thorns and flames).

"Under the left arm of the cross, large letters,
as if of crystal clear water which ran down upon
the altar, formed these words: 'Grace and Mercy.'"

Sr. Lucia understood that this was the Mystery of the Most
Holy Trinity which was shown to her, and she received insights

about this mystery which she was not permitted to reveal. Our Lady then said to her:

> "The moment has come in which God asks the Holy Father, in union with all the Bishops of the world, to make the consecration of Russia to my Immaculate Heart, promising to save it by this means. There are so many souls whom the Justice of God condemns for sins committed against me, that I have come to ask reparation: sacrifice yourself for this intention and pray" (Sister Lucia's *Memoirs*, p. 198).

Later, in an intimate communication, Our Lord complained to Sr. Lucia, saying:

> "They did not wish to heed my request. Like the King of France, they will repent and do it, but it will be too late. Russia will have already spread her errors throughout the world, provoking wars, and persecutions of the Church; the Holy Father will have much to suffer" *(Idem,* p. 464).

Our Lord here is alluding to the promise He made to Louis XIV through St. Margaret Mary Alacoque. Our Lord promised to give the king a life of grace and eternal glory, as well as victory over his enemies, if he would consecrate himself to the Sacred Heart, let It reign in his palace, paint It on his banners, and have It engraved on his coat of arms. Foolishly, Louis ignored Our Lord's request.

In the next century, the godless French Revolution ravaged France. In 1792, King Louis XVI was imprisoned in the Tower of the Temple. There, he recalled the request made to his grandfather. In his hopeless situation, the king then vowed to consecrate himself, his family, and his kingdom to the Sacred Heart of Jesus, if he regained his freedom, the crown, and royal power. God said it was too late. Louis XVI, as everyone knows, left his prison only to go to the guillotine (Borelli, Spann, de Oliveira, *Our Lady of Fatima: Prophecies of Tragedy or Hope. . . ,* p. 83).

On January 11, 1871, while France was being overrun by the Prussians in the disastrous Franco-Prussian War, the French nation finally responded to the request of Our Lord to St. Margaret Mary. The nation vowed to build the Basilica of the Sacred Heart on the Hill of the Martyrs (Montmartre) overlooking Paris. This vow moved the heart of the Blessed Virgin Mary. A week later, she appeared to four children at Portmain and brought them hope with the words: *My Son permits Himself to be moved.* Within ten days the war ended.

At Portmain Our Lady appeared surrounded by forty-three stars. It was a warning to the nation of France that it had 43 years to turn back to the Sacred Heart. It did not. 1871 plus 43 equals the year World War I began.

Nor was this all. People did not listen to Our Lady's request to Sr. Lucia. Russia was not converted. World War II followed and the errors of Russia have spread throughout the world.

How similar John's vision on Patmos is to Sister Lucia's at Tuy. Both had a vision of the Trinity. Both visions involved world events in their own day. As the conquest of Rome in John's day depended in large measure on the early Christians patiently enduring suffering, so the outcome of events in modern history depend in large measure on Christians complying with God's requests given at Fatima and Tuy. As John promised that the blood of martyrs would become a mustard seed, leading to the victory of the Church over the Roman Empire, so Sr. Lucia said God promised the conversion of Russia if the Church would consecrate Russia to Mary's Immaculate Heart.

Indeed, *blessed are those who listen to this prophetic message (Rev. 1:3).*

CHAPTER 7

The Seven Seals
(*Revelation* 6-7)

Chapter 6 of Revelation:
Then I watched while the Lamb broke open the first of the seven seals. The first four seals are broken at once; and they present one picture: the four horsemen of the Apocalypse.

This is probably the best remembered chapter of *Revelation*, precisely because of the four horsemen of Notre Dame. In 1924, when undefeated Notre Dame sank Army 13-7, Grantland Rice labeled the Notre Dame backfield—Harry Stuhldreher, Jim Crowley, Don Miller and Elmer Layden—the "Four Horsemen." Rice wrote:

> "Outlined against a blue-grey October sky the four horsemen rode again. In dramatic lore they are known as famine, pestilence, destruction and death. These are only aliases. Their real names are Stuhldreher, Crowley, Miller and Layden.
> "They formed the crust of the South Bend cyclone before which another fighting Army football team was swept over the precipice of the Polo grounds yesterday afternoon as 55,000 spectators peered down on the bewildering panorama spread on a green plain below" (Francis Wallace, *Knute Rockne*, p. 158).

John borrowed the imagery of the horsemen from the stable of the prophet Zechariah (1:8f; 6:2f). The four horsemen symbolize the havoc wreaked upon people by the godless. The

41

major weapon of godless powers is war, the white horse. War creates bloodshed, the red horse. And if not arrested, war causes famine, the black horse; and death, the pale green horse.

In John's day, the white horse and its rider with bow was an allusion to the Parthians, who invaded the eastern part of the Roman Empire under Nero (62 A.D.), and were victorious. As always, war brings a drop in the standard of living, due to the scarcity of food and a corresponding rise in prices. Thus in the reign of Domitian (92 A.D.), a quart of wheat, or three quarts of barley, the poor people's food, cost a day's wages. Oil and wine were prohibitive, out of reach of everyone but the very rich. Many starved to death.

The first four seals, therefore, reveal that the evils of war, bloodshed, famine and death come, not from God, but from the godless. And God permits such evils not only to move the wicked to repent, but especially to help the just by causing a temporary lull in persecution.

Two men in a forest were fighting against each other, when a bear attacked them. They had to stop fighting each other to defend themselves against the bear. The Parthian invasion, bloodshed, famine, and death gave the Romans other things to think about besides the Christians; and these evils compelled them to turn against the invader instead of persecuting the Christians.

In our day, the four horsemen of the Apocalypse ride again. The twentieth century has been a century of wars; wars of one nation against another; war on innocent babies (abortion, abused children); war on the elderly and the incurable (euthanasia); war against the weak (homelessness, famine); war against our young (chemical dependency, suicide, neglect).

Our Lady said to Fr. Gobbi:

Daily an attack is being made upon life. Each year, throughout the world, innocent children are being slaughtered in their mother's womb and the number of murders, robberies and acts of violence are increasing...

The world is at the mercy of my Adversary, who is ruling it with his spirit of pride and rebellion...leading an immense number...along the road of pleasure, of sin, of disobedience to the laws of God.

Only the powerful force of prayer and reparative penance will be able to save the world from. . .the justice of God (#256).

When the Lamb broke open the fifth seal, John saw the spirits of those who had been martyred because of the word of God, and their witness to it. They, having sacrificed their lives for God, are underneath the altar, the place of sacrifice. They cried out in a loud voice to the One on the throne, "How long, O Master, is this going to go on?" (*Rev.* 6:10). God the Father answers, "Be patient a little while longer. There are others on earth who must fight the good fight and die for the faith (*Rev.* 6:11).

Then the Lamb broke the sixth seal, which foretold the unloosing of elemental disasters: earthquakes, eclipses of the sun and moon, stars falling and the sky disappearing behind thunderclouds, mountains shaken and islands uprooted. All the wicked, found in seven classes of people: kings, nobles, commanders, wealthy, powerful, slave and free, shall be judged.

These will think that this is the end of the world and will try to hide (as Adam and Eve did) from the wrath of the One on the throne and the Lamb. Rather, all this will signal the end of one era and the ushering in of another: the end of Roman paganism and the beginning of the Christian era.

Chapter 7 of Revelation:

Before the breaking of the seventh seal, there is an interlude: two visions.

The first vision is the sealing of the 144,000. John sees four angels at the four corners of the earth—the earth is seen as a table or rectangular surface.[4] They hold back the corner

---

4. Angels have always played a very active part in the working out of salvation history. They are created pure spirits who act as go-betweens God and man. Besides acting as His messengers to us, they are assigned by God to help and guide us in the journey of life. They love us dearly and stand ready to assist us with their powerful help. Devotion to the angels, especially to our guardian angels, must never be neglected.

winds, for these, not the side winds, were considered harm-ful. Another angel comes from the east. Because the sun rises in the east, the east was considered the source of light and the place of paradise. And he tells the other four angels not to harm the earth till he seals the elect.

Sealing denotes ownership, much like the brand on cattle. The seal will not necessarily protect the elect from physical harm, but it will empower them to endure patiently even death and thus secure eternal triumph. 144,000 are sealed; that is, the square of twelve (the number of Israel's tribes), multiplied by a thousand, symbolic of the new Israel which embraces every nation, race, people and tongue. In the list-ing of the twelve tribes, Judah is put first, because of the "Lion of Judah"; and Dan is omitted, because Jewish folklore has it that the anti-Christ would come from the tribe of Dan. The tribe of Joseph fills in for Dan.

The second vision shifts from earth to Heaven. Of those sealed, a huge crowd is saved. They come from the four corners of the earth, symbolized by four groups: nations, races, peo-ples, tongues. They confess that their victory over their trials on earth was due to the One on the throne and the Lamb. All the angels, standing around the throne, the elders and the four creatures, concur and say, "Amen."

One of the elders asks John who are all these people dressed in white. John answers that the elder should know better than himself. The elder does know better; his answer epitomizes the message of the book: *These are the ones who have sur-vived the time of great distress* (the fierce persecution by the Romans); *they have washed their robes and made them white in the blood of the Lamb.* In other words, their patient endur-ance under trial has brought them before God's throne.

There, before God, they will never hunger nor thirst, never be scorched by the sun; for the Lamb will shepherd them, bringing them to life-giving waters and wiping away every tear from their eyes.

What a strong motivation this picture is! When Hannibal was crossing the Alps, he spurred his soldiers on through the ice and snow by constantly reminding them: "Post Alpes, Italia"—"After the Alps, the sunny climes of Italy."

So John reminds the persecuted: "After death, life—eternal, painless, ever-joyful! Therefore, do not despair. Do not fall apart. Do not say, 'What's the use?' Be patient. The Lord has sealed you at baptism. He loves you. He has conquered death by His resurrection. Endure!"

Chapter 8:1
When the Lamb opens the seventh seal, there is a silence in Heaven for about half an hour. It is the calm before the storm. Seven angels are given seven trumpets to announce the disasters to come. So great shall these be that there is awe, a hush, a silence!

England's great poet, John Keats, always wanted to read the epic poetry of Homer; but Keats could not read Greek. When Chapman translated Homer from the Greek into English, Keats devoured Homer's classic epic poetry. He stayed up all night reading it. The next morning, he composed a sonnet expressing the joy of his discovery.

Then felt I like some watcher of the skies
When a new planet swims into his ken;
Or like stout Cortez (Balboa), when with eagle eyes
He stared at the Pacific—and all his men
Looked at each other with a wild surmise—
SILENT, upon a peak in Darien."

When the Lamb broke open the seventh seal, there was silence in heaven for about a half an hour. (Rev. 8:1)

CHAPTER 8

The Seven Trumpets
(*Revelation* 8-9)

The seventh seal introduces the seven trumpets. The seven trumpets announce disasters. A minor liturgy in Heaven show that these disasters are in answer to the prayers of the faithful on earth.

An angel bears these prayers in a golden censer before the throne of God. Just as the prayers of the Hebrews in Egypt brought down God's plagues upon the Egyptians, so the prayers of God's holy ones, rising up to God in an envelope of perfumed incense, bring down the wrath of God upon those persecuting His children. "I've heard the afflictions of my people," God told Moses at the burning bush. And the angel hurls the censer filled with burning coals down to the earth to signify that God has also heard the prayers of His holy ones.

Each divine intervention of God is introduced with a trumpet blast. Tat-a-tat: here comes God! Pay attention!

The first four trumpets (8:6-12), like the first four seals, make one impression. They usher in four plagues that afflict the material universe directly and evildoers indirectly: 1. the land by hail and fire; 2. the salt water by volcanic earthquakes; 3 the fresh water by Wormwood turning it bitter; and 4. the sky by being darkened by eclipses of the sun and moon and stars. The four plagues are a replay of some of the plagues in Egypt (*Ex.* 10). They affect only one third of creation; therefore they are not announcing the end of the world, but the end of an era—of paganism. As the plagues of Egypt led God's people to freedom, so once again God's disasters will eventually liberate Christians from Roman persecutions.

It is significant that the Ukrainian word for wormwood (a bitter wild herb used as a tonic in rural Russia) is Chernobyl! Many Russians have seen in the nuclear disaster at Chernobyl, a fulfillment of this passage from Revelation. The disaster contaminated land and poisoned water for over 1,000 square miles.

Following these disasters, a solitary eagle flying high in the sky cries out three times in a loud voice: *Woe, Woe! Woe to the inhabitants of the earth from the rest of the trumpet blasts that the three angels are about to blow* (8:13). Woe!—because the last three plagues will be especially grievous and afflict all the "inhabitants of the earth," that is, those who are not God-fearing.

The first woe, **the fifth trumpet** (*Rev.* 9:1-12), predicts diabolical attacks against the human race, like a scourge of locusts on crops. These attacks will harm, but not kill, people. (The second woe, the sixth trumpet, representing another kind of diabolical attack: an invasion by the Parthians, living east of the Euphrates, will bring death.)

The one responsible for the plague begun at the blowing of the fifth trumpet is Lucifer, the star fallen from Heaven. Another name for him is *Abaddon*, which means the destroyer or ruiner, which the devil is. He is given the key to the abyss, for he can do nothing without God's permission. Nor can the demons of Hell do anything, unless God lets them out. When Lucifer lets them out, all Hell breaks loose, a veritable Pandora's box is opened.

Yet their destructive power is in the hands of God. And the length of time given them to wreak their evil on mankind is limited to the life-span of a locust, namely, to five months, a very short time.

Locusts aptly symbolize the ferocity of the demons. The seers of Medjugorje, who saw Hell, state that the demons and the damned had the appearances of horrible, nightmarish creatures. John implies the same thing in his description of the demons (*Rev.* 9:7-11). They looked like horses with human faces, had hair like women's hair, chests like iron breastplates, and tails like scorpions. In a word, their appearance is horrific, grotesque and fearsome.

A locust plague is one of the most dreaded scourges in the East. In the 19th century, locusts hit Algeria, and 200,000 people starved to death. Generally, locusts attack crops; but the locust-like demons are forbidden to touch the crops. Their harmful activity is restricted only to those who have not been sealed by the angel. And even in this instance, they are not allowed to kill them. Yet so great will be the suffering that the afflicted will want to die; but they will be unable.

The sixth trumpet (9:13-21) ushers in the second woe. At its blowing, a voice came from the altar of incense, to remind God's people that these divine interventions were the result of their sacrifices and prayers. The voice said to the trumpeter, *Release the four angels who are bound at the banks of the great river Euphrates.* Beyond the Euphrates used to lie the great Empires of Assyria and Babylon. As armies came from these lands beyond the Euphrates to punish a disobedient Israel, so a more ferocious enemy would arise to punish a godless Roman world.

This dreaded enemy was Parthia, east of the Euphrates. The Parthians rode white horses. Their battle strategy was to retreat, then stop suddenly, face their pursuing foes, and fire deadly arrows at them. This effective maneuver gave rise to the expression "Parthian shot," which means a deadly blow to which there is no possible answer. That is why John said, *Their horses have tails like snakes with heads that inflict harm.*

Yet the rest of the unsealed who were not killed by these plagues did not repent. As the plagues of Egypt only hardened the Pharaoh's heart, so the survivors of these plagues did not give up the worship of demons nor repent of their wicked deeds.

Part II

A. Introduction: Christ In His Legate And Witnesses
(*Revelation* 10-11)

CHAPTER 9

Christ's Legate and Witnesses
(*Revelation* 10-11)

Before the breaking of the seventh seal, there was an interlude of two visions: 1. the marking of the 144,000 on earth and, 2. the elect before the heavenly throne. So too here, before the blowing of the seventh trumpet, there is an interlude of two visions: 1. the angel with the scroll, and 2. the two witnesses.

Chapter 10 of Revelation
The angel with the small scroll (10:1-13). John sees a mighty angel come down from Heaven. This angel is the legate of Christ. Hence he is of epic proportions: he is wrapped in a cloud with a halo around his head; his legs are like pillars of fire, for he is immovable; in his hand is a little scroll, for only a small part of God's plan for the world is to be revealed; it is not sealed like the big scroll in chapter 5. Like a colossus, the angel stands astride sea and land—one foot on land and one on sea, for his message is to all the world; so his voice is like the roar of a lion. God in a voice of seven thunders ratifies the angel's message. What it is we do not know, for John is forbidden to write it down.

Then the angel took an oath and promised that God would no longer delay; that after the seventh trumpet, His kingdom would come on earth.

Next, he ordered John to eat the scroll; that is, to digest the message, know it completely so that he could give the

51

message to all. It was a bittersweet message. Sweet, because it predicted the final victory of God's people; bitter, because it announced their sufferings. Sweet to the faithful; bitter to the unfaithful. Sweet to hear, but hard to heed.

Chapter 11 of Revelation
The two witnesses (11:1-14). Abruptly, the scene changes: John is told to measure the heavenly temple.

The temple is the Church. The measuring of the temple suggests that God will preserve the faithful remnant who remain true to Christ. Hence salvation is to be found in the Church. Outside the temple are the godless Gentiles who will persecute the Church for three and a half years (42 months or 1260 days). The vicious persecution of the Jews by Antiochus IV Epiphanes (171-168 B.C.) in the time of the Maccabees lasted three and one half years (June 168-December 165 B.C.). Thus 3-1/2 years or 42 months or 1260 days became the prototype of the periods of persecution of God's people. These numbers signified that the life of the Church, viewed as being persecuted, is a comparatively short time compared to eternity.

During these times of persecution, the Church will give witness to the faith through her martyrs (*Acts* 1:8). They are spoken of as two witnesses, because in Deuteronomy (19:15), a judicial fact can be established only on the testimony of two or three witnesses. They are called two olive trees and two lampstands, because they act as leaders of the Church. As Moses gave witness before Pharaoh by turning the Nile to blood, and Elijah gave witness before Israel by preventing rain to fall, so God's martyrs will give witness during the entire period of persecution and thus build up the Church.

When they have finished their work, the beast from the bottomless pit, the Emperor Nero, will war against them and kill them. As in Jerusalem Christ was crucified, so in the new Jerusalem, pagan Rome—a Sodom of immorality and an

Egypt of oppression—the Christians will be martyred and slain. And the ultimate insult heaped upon them will be not to bury them (*Ps.* 79:3; *Tobit* 1:16f).

The earth's inhabitants will rejoice to be rid of those who pricked their consciences by their lives and message. But their merriment will be shortlived; after three and a half days, the martyrs will be vindicated, as blazing triumph follows upon apparent defeat. The Church's triumph, coupled with elemental disasters like earthquakes, that kill large numbers, will at last terrify the rest into giving glory to God.

Then **the seventh angel** (11:15-18) blows his trumpet and God's kingdom is ushered in by the Edict of Toleration of Constantine the Great (313 A.D.). The triumph of the Church is a perennial thing. Again and again, the Church, like Christ, will be crucified and buried, but will rise again and again. The gates of Hell will not prevail against her. Christ reigns in His Church as the Lamb slain, yet standing triumphant. *Christus vincit, Christus regnat, Christus imperat.* "Christ conquers, Christ reigns, Christ rules." Julian the Apostate, who had tried to overthrow Christianity, was at last forced to admit: "Thou hast conquered, O pale Galilaean!"

And the twenty-four elders once more acknowledge God's judgment.

Chapter 11 (14-19) is a summary of the rest of the book (Chs. 12-22), namely, the coming of the reign of God after the victory over the powers of Hell.

It is put within the seventh trumpet to link Part 1 (Chs. 4-9) and Part 2 (Chs. 12-22) together.

Part 1 is negative: it deals with the trials and sufferings of the Church and the punishment of the wicked.

Part 2 is positive: the Church will not be vanquished, rather Satan will be chained and the wicked finally judged.

Part II

B. The Church Triumphant
(*Revelation* 12-22)

CHAPTER 10

The Woman and the Dragon
(*Revelation* 12)

After the series of preparatory visions of Chapters 10-11, a new septette begins—**the Seven Signs.** God's temple is opened and John sees the ark of the covenant (11:19).

The temple is God's Church and the Ark of the Covenant symbolizes His presence in the midst of His people, to guard and protect them as did the Ark of the Covenant in the Exodus. That presence today is the Blessed Sacrament. The series of signs that follow introduce the members of the cast in the drama to be enacted between good and evil.

1. The first sign is that of the **woman.** *A great sign appeared in the sky, a woman, clothed with the sun, with the moon beneath her feet, and on her head a crown of twelve stars (Rev.* 12:1).

The Woman symbolized Israel, God's people in the Old Testament—the Israel that gave birth to the Messiah. In John's day, she symbolized the new Israel, the early Church, suffering persecution from the dragon, Domitian.

For us today, the woman symbolizes Our Lady,[5] as she herself told Fr. Stefano Gobbi repeatedly. *I am the Woman clothed with the sun who has the task of fighting against the Red Dragon*

---

5. At the present time the Church is investigating apparitions in San Nicolás, Argentina. There, Our Lady has stated to the seer: "I am the new Ark of the Covenant! I am the Woman clothed with the Sun."

and his powerful army, to conquer him, to bind him and drive him away into his kingdom of death, that Christ alone may reign over the world. (#414).

The sun that clothes the Woman is the Trinity. She is bathed in their blinding light, for she is daughter of the Father, who had her conceived immaculate; she is the bride of the Holy Spirit; and she is the Mother of Jesus, the Son of God.

The Woman wears a crown, the sign of her royalty, for she is Queen-Mother, scion of King David and Mother of the King of kings.

The twelve stars represent the 12 tribes of Israel, of which she, as the mother of the Messiah, is the honor and glory.

They also signify the 12 apostles, who are the foundation-stones of the new Israel, the Church. She is their Queen, for she mothered them not only during the life of her divine Son, but especially after His Ascension.

But the twelve stars further signify all the Christians in John's day, struggling against persecution.

In our own day, the twelve signify all the other apostles of these last times: all those who consecrate themselves to her Immaculate Heart, who allow themselves to be guided by her in order to fight the Red Dragon and gain the ultimate victory, as did the early Christians (#414).

The Woman was in labor pains to give birth to a child: in John's day, to the birth of a Christian civilization and the death of paganism; and in our day, to beget Marian apostles, who will form part of her victorious army against the Red Dragon.

When God wanted to give birth to a new people in the Americas in 1531, He sent His Mother to Guadalupe, outside Mexico City. There she was clothed with the sun, with a crescent moon under her feet, and with her garments besprinkled with stars. Significantly, she wore the maternity belt commonly used by the native women of that day, for she was about to give birth to a new people in the Americas.

2. The second sign is that of the **dragon.** *Then another sign appeared in the sky: it was a huge red dragon with seven heads and ten horns, and on its head were seven diadems* (*Rev.* 12:3).

In John's day, the huge Red Dragon was pagan Rome, seated on seven hills; and the ten horns were the ten Emperors, who ruled Rome: Tiberius (14-37), Caligula (37-41), Claudius (41-54), Nero (54-68), Galba, Otto, Vitellius, Vespasian (69-79), Titus (79-81) and Domitian (81-96). Only seven had diadems, for Galba, Otto, and Vitellius were assassinated before they could reign.

In our day, Our Lady told Fr. Gobbi: *The huge Red Dragon is atheistic communism which has spread everywhere the error of the denial and of the obstinate rejection of God.* It has ten horns using its power of communication *to lead humanity to disobey the ten commandments of God* (#404).

In the Bible, horns do not refer to animals, but to trumpets that amplify the voice, like bullhorns. In our day, the ten horns refer to the means of communication: the media, radio, television. Most of these instruments of communication are in the hands of the enemies of God, and they are being used to lead humanity to break the ten commandments (#405). In 1982, Our Lady told Fr. Gobbi: *Immorality is spreading like a flood of filth and is being propagated by the means of social communication, especially the cinema, the press and television* (#256).

The huge Red Dragon has succeeded. . .in conquering humanity with the error of . . . atheism, which has now seduced all the nations of the earth. It has succeeded in building up . . . a new civilization without God, materialistic, egoistic, hedonistic, arid and cold, which carries within itself the seeds of corruption and of death (#404).

The aim of the Red Dragon is to draw all humanity away from glorifying the Most Holy Trinity. It seeks to obscure the work of the Father—which is <u>creation</u>—by spreading atheism to a degree never before known. It seeks to bedim the work of the Son, which is His <u>Church</u>, by spreading error and infidelity in her like a cancer. It blocks the work of the Holy Spirit, which is <u>sanctification</u>, by causing a loss of a sense of sin in countless souls through the neglect of the sacrament of reconciliation (#200).

Its tail swept away a third of the stars in the sky and hurled them down to the earth (Rev. 12:4). In John's day, this was Cerinthus and the Nicolaitans. In our day, it is those religious who oppose the Papacy. Our Lady laments: *The scandal, even of bishops who do not obey the Vicar of my Son and who sweep a great number of my poor children along the path of error. . . wounds my heart* (#106). *Secularism has stricken the life of many priests and religious* (#390).

So the Woman is clothed with the sun of the Trinity to restore to its splendor the work of creation, of redemption, and of sanctification, in such a way that the Most Holy Trinity will receive glory once more from all. Our Lady has begun the great battle and wills to wage it through her faithful children—who form her heel, the heel that will crush the head of "the serpent, who is called the Devil and Satan" (#408).

3. The third sign is that of **the Dragon against the Woman's Child.** The dragon stood before the Woman to devour her child, Jesus. But the risen Jesus ascended into Heaven. The Church He has left behind fled into the desert, the prover-bial place of God's protection, as in the Exodus. The Church is protected by God during her entire sojourn on desert earth (1260 days), which will be one of constant warfare with the dragon (*Rev.* 12:4-6).

The dragon's hatred of Jesus was so great that when he saw Jesus ascending into Heaven, the dragon pursued Him, still not knowing of His divinity. But Michael and his angels battled against the dragon and his angels and hurled them down to the earth; they fell like lightning from the sky (*Lk.* 10:18).

Then a loud voice in Heaven proclaimed, perhaps to the

glorified martyrs who had watched the battle, that no more would they have to fear, *for the accuser of our brothers is cast out.* Many of the martyrs had been caught and executed because someone had informed on them to the Roman authorities for the sake of money.

So, the one with a loud voice calls them to rejoice, for now they are secure and need fear no more denunciations; and because their salvation was due to the blood of the Lamb, which had given them courage to sacrifice their lives for the faith.

After Satan has been cast out of Heaven, all that is left for him is a short time (from the Ascension of Jesus to His Second Coming) during which he can vent his fury on this earth before he is finally destroyed. In this, his last death struggle, the ragings of Satan are terrible. *Woe to you, earth and sea, for the devil has come down to you in great fury, for he knows he has but a short time. (Rev. 12:12).*

4. The fourth sign is that of **the Dragon against the Woman herself.** Having failed in his attack on the Woman's child, the dragon, the ancient serpent, attacks the Woman herself.

In John's day, the Woman was the Church, harassed and bitterly persecuted by the dragons, Nero and Domitian. Nero's persecution was restricted to the city of Rome; Domitian extended over the entire Roman Empire. Nero was an insane devil; Domitian was worse—a sane devil.

In our own day, the Woman is Mary, the Mother of the Church. The dragon has attacked her by trying to denigrate devotion to her.

In many places of worship the images of the saints have been removed, even those of your heavenly Mother (#270).

How deeply saddened I am by the fact that I am, so frequently today, ousted from the churches. Sometimes, I am placed outside, in a corridor, like some trinket; sometimes I am put in the back of the church, so that none of my children can venerate me (#283).

But the woman was given the two wings of the great eagle so she could fly to her place in the desert, where. . .she was taken care of for a year, two years and a half-year (Rev. 12:14).

In John's day, the eagle, swift and strong, symbolized the swift and powerful help of God in behalf of His Church. The wings are the word of God heard and lived, the faith and charity of the early Christians. The desert symbolized the protection of God for His Church, all during her earthly sojourn (3-1/2 years).

In our day, Our Lady told Fr. Gobbi, *The great eagle is the word of God. . .Of the four Gospels, the eagle indicates that of St. John.* The two wings are the word of God, *received, loved and kept with faith. . .and lived with grace and charity.* (#403). *The desert, in which I have made my habitual dwelling place, is made up of the hearts and souls of those children who receive me, who listen to me, who entrust themselves to me, who consecrate themselves to my Immaculate Heart. . .I am working forcefully that they believe in the Gospel, be guided only by the wisdom of the Gospel, be ever the Gospel lived out. . .that they may become courageous witnesses of faith and luminous examples of holiness* (#403).

The serpent, however, spewed a torrent of water out of his mouth, to destroy the Woman *(Rev. 12:15).*

In John's day, this torrent was the lies spread about the Christians. They were libeled as treasonous, because they would not worship the Emperor as Lord and God. They were accused of cannibalism, because they ate flesh and drank blood.

In our day, this torrent is the collection of new theological doctrines against Mary, the Woman. On December 10, 1925, Our Lady asked Sr. Lucia, the last surviving seer of the Fatima apparitions, to make known the devotion of the Five First Saturdays. On the first Saturdays of five consecutive months, Our Lady asked that her children go to Confession, receive Holy Communion, recite 5 decades of the Rosary, and spend 15 minutes in front of the Blessed Sacrament meditating on the mysteries of the Rosary—all with the intention of making reparation to her Immaculate Heart.

She called for reparation because of the five blasphemies committed against her Immaculate Heart. These are the denial of her Immaculate Conception; the denial of her perpetual virginity; the denial of her divine maternity; the implanting in the hearts of children indifference, contempt and even hatred for their Immaculate Mother; and downgrading her by removing her statues from churches (#180, #379).

But the earth helped the woman and swallowed the torrent spewed from the dragon's mouth" (Rev. 12:16). Apathy can cut both ways: just as the good can be indifferent to promoting good, so the bad can be indifferent to promoting evil. The Woman is aided by earthlings who do not cooperate with the dragon, because of their inertia.

Foiled again, *the dragon. . .went off to wage war against the rest of the woman's offspring, namely, those who keep God's commandments and bear witness to Jesus (Rev. 12:17).*

Despite his furious onslaught, Our Lady (through Fr. Gobbi) urges us: *Bear within yourselves the witness of Jesus in these times of purification in order to walk along the road of fidelity to Christ and his Church, and of an ever greater holiness. . .*

Bear within yourselves the witness of Jesus in these times of apostasy in order to be strong and courageous witnesses of faith. For this, I invite you to be ever more united to the Pope, to sustain him with your prayer and with your love, to accept and spread his teaching. . .

Maintain the witness of Jesus in these times of the great tribulation. The days foretold by the Gospel and the Apocalypse have arrived. The forces of evil, united by the power of the one who opposes himself to Christ. . .will be unloosed to seduce a great part of humanity (#408).

In his fury against the witnesses of Jesus and those who keep the commandments of God, the dragon will enroll the help of two other beasts, like himself, to wage war against them: a beast from the sea and a beast from the land.

CHAPTER 11

The Two Beasts and the Lamb
(*Revelation* 13-14:5)

5. The fifth sign: the Sea Beast. *Then I saw a beast come out of the sea with ten horns and seven heads; on its horns were ten diadems, and on its heads blasphemous name(s)* (13:1).

The wild beast come out of the sea is the political arm of the Roman Empire: the proconsuls of Rome, endowed with the authority to enforce Emperor worship. The blasphemous name on its heads is "Caesar is Lord and God." The beast is monstrous: cruel and cunning like a leopard, strong as a bear, and ferocious as a lion. The head wounded is Nero "come alive" again in Domitian, a second Nero. Nero was insane; Domitian was demonic. Many give in to this Emperor worship just to get along, or just because they think you can't fight City Hall (*Rev.* 13:2-4).

What John is telling the Christians of his day is that you cannot eradicate evil entirely. As Christ died and rose again, so will evil: it may be snuffed out for a time but it will surely be resurrected again and again. Like a weed, you can kill evil, but not for good. It will resurface.

The beast exercises its authority for 42 months—the whole lifetime of the Church on earth. In every age Caesar tries to take over the things of God, like divine worship. The inhabitants of the earth yield, but not those whose names are written in the book of life. They endure faithfully, even though fidelity to Christ might mean captivity or death (*Rev.* 13:5-10).

Mary tells us that the dragon in our day is Marxist atheism and the beast is Freemasonry. Freemasonry (beyond the 33rd degree) honors a deity: "The Great Architect of the Universe." A mason is a builder. Masonry is building a temple or a city.

But the temple is not to the true God, for Masonry rejects the cornerstone, Jesus Christ, and the rock foundation of His temple, the Papacy. And the city it seeks to build is not the city of God, but the secular city, the city without God (See, Randall Paine, *His Time Is Short: The Devil and His Agenda*, pp. 52-55).

Our Lady told Fr. Gobbi: *These are therefore the times when a civilization without God is being constructed and all humanity is being led to live without Him* (#409).

It was Freemasonry that took the eldest daughter of the Church, France, away from Christianity. Carlton J.H. Hayes, renowned historian, wrote: "In France, where Freemasonry was frankly atheistic in principle and practical tendency, almost every Radical politician was a Freemason" *(A Political and Cultural History of Modern Europe*, Vol. 2, fn. 555).

Men like Garibaldi, Jules Ferry (who concocted the infamous Laic Laws [1881] that secularized the schools of France), Aristide Briand, George Clemenceau, and Emile Combes (a very active Freemason and doctrinaire radical, who rigorously enforced the Association Laws, which sought to nationalize all church property), created a godless France. (Hayes, *Idem* vol. 2, p. 564).

In our own country, Franklin Delano Roosevelt and Harry S. Truman, both 33rd degree Masons, packed the United States Supreme Court with Masonic judges. From 1941 to 1971, there were never less than five Masonic judges on the Court. And in those critical thirty years, these judges did to America what was done to 19th century France: they secularized this once God-fearing America by raw judicial power (Paul Fisher,

Behind the Lodge Door, pp. 131-134, 160f, 255-59, Appendix A). This Masonic Court outlawed prayer in schools, repeatedly denied aid to private schools, legitimized pornography, abortion, and so on.

The beast is like a leopard—cunning and sly. It has ten horns, like the dragon. But, unlike the dragon, the crowns were on the horns, not on the heads. For the dragon uses the heads of government to endorse its evils; but the beast uses the horns of the mass media to broadcast its godless ideas.

God gave the ten commandments; but Masonic judges put their judicial decrees above the laws of God. Our Lady told Fr. Gobbi: *If the Lord communicated His law with the ten commandments, Freemasonry spreads everywhere, through the power of its ten horns, a law which is completely opposed to that of God* (#405).

To the seven virtues (the three theological and four cardinal virtues) this Humanism counters with the seven capital vices. To faith it opposes pride; to hope, lust; to charity, avarice; to prudence, anger; to fortitude, sloth; to justice, envy; to temperance, gluttony. Whoever becomes a victim of the seven capital vices is gradually led to make these vices gods. Hence the blasphemous names on every head of the beast.

To counterattack, the Woman (Mary) is training her children to observe the ten commandments of God, to make frequent use of the sacraments, especially penance and Holy Communion, to practice the virtues vigorously. In this way, the children of Mary, her heel, will unmask the subtle snares of the beast like a leopard (#405).

6. **The sixth sign: the Land Beast.** *Then I saw another beast come out of the earth; it had two horns like a lamb's, but spoke like a dragon* (13:11).

The "beast come out of the earth" represents the religious

arm of the pagan Roman Empire. The two horns symbolize
that arm, for the Jewish high priest wore on his head a miter
with two horns. And the lamb has always been the symbol
of sacrifice, for instance, the paschal lamb and the Lamb of
God. So the beast with two horns like a lamb's represented
the priests of pagan Rome. The beast spoke like a dragon,
for the priests of pagan Rome had the authority of the Emperor
behind them. And they compelled the earth and its inhabitants to worship the first beast—the State.

In their worship services, they tried to mimic the miracles
of the saints of God. Like the wizard in the Wizard of Oz,
they had fire belch out from their idols; by ventriloquism,
they had their idols speak—it was a coverup for their nothingness and a ruse to force Emperor worship upon the people (*Rev.* 13:13-15).

Those who joined in the worship were stamped, on their
hands or their foreheads, with the number of the beast, 666.
Without this stamp, they would suffer economic loss, could
not buy or sell. The hand expresses human activity; the forehead indicates the mind. The person who follows the beast
will act and think like it. He will make money his god, pleasure his sole pursuit in life, and self as the center of all his
actions. He will accept atheism and deny and reject God.
He is, in a word, a materialist and a secularist (#410).

In our day, the beast with the two horns like a lamb indicates anti-Catholic infiltration into the Catholic Church herself. Our Lady, with bleeding heart, cried out to Fr. Gobbi:
*There has also entered into the Church disunity, division, strife
and antagonism. The forces of atheism and Masonry, having
infiltrated within it, are on the point of breaking up its interior
unity and of darkening the splendor of its sanctity* (#332).

Jesus Christ is the way, the truth and the life. He is the
way to life by His truth. Masonry works to obscure His divine
word by natural and rational interpretations of the Scriptures,
by emptying the mysteries of faith of all mystery, to make
them more acceptable (#406, #411; see Paine, *Idem*, pp. 73-76).

In this way, it seeks to destroy the historical Christ. Next, it seeks to destroy the mystical Christ, the Church. It seeks to do this by a false ecumenism that accepts all religions as equally good, by denying the real presence of Christ in the Eucharist, by suppressing all external signs that indicate the real presence, like no genuflections, no lights or flowers surrounding the Blessed Sacrament, shunting the Blessed Sacrament to some corner of the church (#406).

The Woman (identified in Genesis) asks her children to oppose this force of evil by consecrating themselves to her, by renewing their devotion to Jesus in the Eucharist, and by being one with the Pope.

One who understands can calculate the number of the beast, for it is a number that stands for a person. His number is 666 (Rev. 13:18).

Six is the number of imperfection. Tripled, it stands for the highest imperfection. In John's day, the number stood for "Caesar Nero."

In our day, Our Lady said, *The number 333 indicates the divinity. Lucifer rebels against God through pride, because he wants to put himself above God. He who wants to put himself above God bears the sign 666, and consequently this number indicates the name of Satan... him who sets himself against Christ, of the Antichrist* (#407).

In 666 A.D., a new attack against Christianity came through the phenomenon of Islam, which denies the Trinity and divinity of Christ.[6] By military force, Islam sought to destroy Christianity. It was only through the intervention of the Woman,

---

6. Mohammed (570-632) preached there is one God, Allah, and Mohammed is His greatest prophet. Mohammed taught that God, like a dictator, stamped each man with his fate. Mohammed believed in predestination. That is why his religion is called **Islam**, which means "resignation to the decrees of God."

His followers are called **Moslems**, which means "those who have surrendered to God."

The basic principles which they are to follow are contained in the **Koran**, the book of Mohammed's sayings, compiled after his death.

for whose intervention the Holy Father earnestly prayed, that it did not succeed.

666 doubled is 1332 A.D. In this period of history (1300-1450 A.D.), scholastic philosophy declined and pagan philosophies revived. Our Lady told Fr. Gobbi: *Through the philosophers who begin to give exclusive value to science and then to reason, there is a gradual tendency to constitute human intelligence alone as the sole criterion of truth. There come to birth the great philosophical errors which continue through the centuries down to your days* (#407). With the Protestant Reformation, Tradition was rejected and Scripture alone, privately interpreted, was accepted as the sole rule of faith. This led to the fragmentation of the Church.

666 multiplied by three is 1998 A.D. Our Lady also told Fr. Gobbi: *In this period, Freemasonry...will suceed in... setting up an idol to put in the place of Christ and of his Church. A false christ and a false church.* (#407). This will lead to a great apostasy.

The dragon and the beast come out from the sea and the beast comes out of the earth—these three form a diabolical trinity to oppose the Divine Trinity.

7. The seventh sign: the Lamb and His companions. To combat this trinity of evil, there comes paradoxically the Lamb. *I looked and there was the Lamb standing on Mt. Zion and with him a hundred and forty-four thousand who had his name and his Father's name written on their foreheads (Rev. 14:1).*

The Lamb was standing, because the Church is in the throes of persecution. He who sits at the Father's right hand, stands when the Church is in need of help. Thus during his martyrdom, Stephen saw Christ standing, not sitting (*Acts* 7:51).

And with Him were one hundred and forty-four thousand with the seal of the Lamb and the Father on their foreheads.

One hundred and forty-four thousand is the square of twelve (the number of the tribes of Israel) multiplied by a thousand, symbol of the new Israel, the Church.

The seal of the Lamb is their virginity, in the sense that

they had never defiled themselves by indulging in idolatrous worship, which generally included sacred prostitution, nor by compromising their allegiance to Christ by rationalizing Emperor worship—*on their lips no deceit has been found. They are unblemished* (14:5).

Then John heard a sound from Heaven. It must have been the voice of God, for it was accompanied by a peal of thunder. The voice had power, like the sound of rushing waters. It was melodious, like the sound of many harps. The voice was a call to sing a new hymn for joy, that this throng of 144,000 was but the first fruits of all those yet to be redeemed by the Lamb. Others, many others, were to follow. Alleluia!

ALPHA AND OMEGA
WITH CROWN
(The Lord)

The Lord God says,
"I am the Alpha and the Omega,
the One who is and who was and who is to come,
the Almighty!"
Rev. 1:8

CHAPTER 12

The Seven Angels of Judgment
(Revelation 14:6-20)

The three angels (*Rev.* 14:6-12).
God wants everyone to be saved. So John has a vision of three angels. They appeal to all people, even to pagan Rome, to return to God or else.

The first angel, flying high in the sky, announces the gospel, the everlasting good news, to every nation, tribe, tongue and people. John calls the wicked to repent, for judgment is near.

The second angel warns the city of pagan Rome itself. Give heed to the rudder or give heed to the rocks. He sings a dirge over the new Babylon[7] (pagan Rome), as already fallen, so certain is its destruction if it continues on its course of persecuting the Church.

The third angel holds out the punishment of the wicked and the reward of the good. He warns those who worship the beast or its image, that any cooperation or connivance with the religious demands of emperor cult will be punished with everlasting torments: *Anyone who worships the beast or its image. . .will drink the wine of God's fury: a fire. . .that torments. . .forever.* (*Rev.* 14:10-11).

---

7. The old Babylon under Nabuchadnezzar, who destroyed the temple of Jerusalem (586 B.C.) and led God's chosen people into slavery for 70 years (in what is now modern Iraq), was used by John as the symbol of pagan Rome under Domitian (96 A.D.), persecuting God's Church. The word Babylon was used as a symbol of everything evil.

Hell can be a deterrent. The fires of Hell have lit the way to Heaven for more than one sinner.

Though Hell fire may be a deterrent, Heaven's rewards can be a stimulant. Thus a voice from Heaven said, *Write this: Blessed are the dead who die in the Lord from now on. Yes, said the Spirit, let them find rest from their labors, for their works accompany them* (14:13).

The four angels (14:14-20).
The three angels had warned about a judgment to come: eternal rest or everlasting fire.

The next four angels portray the final judgment, which takes place in two stages: first the wheat; then the grapes.

An angel appears seated on a cloud, looking like a son of man, with a gold crown on his head and a sharp sickle in his hand. He is like a son of man, because he comes to do the work of the Son of Man: to judge. But since no one knows the time or hour of judgment, a second angel comes out of the temple and announces that the time has come. In a loud voice, therefore, he cries out to the one on the cloud to use his sickle and reap the harvest (*Mk.* 4:29). Reaping the harvest symbolizes the gathering of the elect.

A third angel appears out of the temple in Heaven. And he too has a sickle in his hand. But he cannot use it until a fourth angel appears and orders him to use it. This angel comes from the altar, as if in answer to the prayers of God's saints. He orders the third angel to cut clusters of grapes from the vine and tread them in the winepress—a symbol of the doom of the ungodly.

In 1861, Julia Ward Howe, on a visit to some army camps, heard the soldiers singing a grim chant, "John Brown's Body," to the tune of a camp-meeting hymn, "Say, Brothers, Will You Meet Us?" Deeply moved, she later wrote the sturdy words of the "Battle Hymn of the Republic," one of the most stirring poems to come out of the Civil War. She saw the war as the judgment of God on the nation for its terrible sin of slavery and she expressed this judgment in the imagery of Revelation: *He is trampling out the vintage where the grapes of wrath are stored (Rev. 14:10).*

The judgment in Revelation takes place outside the city, on all those who are hostile to God's people. It will be a bloody carnage, of cosmic proportions: blood bridle high, spread around for 200 miles, the length of Palestine. *For a cup is in the Lord's hand, full of spiced and foaming wine, And he pours out from it; even to the dregs they shall drain it; all the wicked of the earth shall drink (Ps. 75:9).*

CHAPTER 13

The Judgment: The Seven Last Plagues
(*Revelation* 15-16)

Having described the harvesting of the just and the unjust, John now details what will happen at that time.

Chapter 15
He begins, *Then I saw in Heaven another sign . . . seven angels with the seven last plagues,* through which God will vent His fury on evil (*Rev.* 15:1).

The emphasis is on the triumph of the just which is necessarily bound up with the punishment of the unjust. Therefore, before the unfolding of the seven plagues, John turns to those who had won the victory over the beast. They are standing on a sea of glass mingled with fire. In their hands they hold harps and sing the songs of Moses and the Lamb.

The sea of glass implies that God sees all that happens on earth. It is mingled with fire to point out that faith is purified in the fire of suffering and that perhaps many of those who had won the victory over the beast had been martyred by fire. The hymn itself harkens back to Moses' canticle after the crossing of the Red Sea (*Ex.* 15:1). It concludes on the hopeful note that, *all nations will come and worship you, for your righteous acts have been revealed* (*Rev.* 15:4).

Then John saw the tent of testimony, like the tabernacle in the desert (*Ex.* 40:34), open up in Heaven. Seven angels with the seven plagues come out of the temple. They are dressed in clean white linen with a gold sash around their chests—like priests.

One of the four living creatures gives the seven angels seven gold bowls filled with the fury of God. Then the temple became so filled with the smoke from God's glory and might that no one could enter it until the seven plagues had been accomplished. The implication is that nothing now can halt the anger of God's vengeance (15:5-8).

On the feast of Yom Kippur, the high priest would enter the Holy of Holies with a bowl of blood to sprinkle on the propitiatory to reconcile the people and God. Here it seems that God refuses all petitions now and throws the bowls of blood in the face of those offering them—the wicked, who "sanctify" their wickedness as religion: emperor worship.

Chapter 16
Having received the seven bowls of God's fury, the seven angels are told to pour them out upon the earth (*Rev.* 16:1).

Since the seven bowls is the only septette that is all gloom, John races through them. One plague follows the other in rapid succession; the only pause is before the last plague as in the other septettes.

All seven plagues are modeled on the plagues of Egypt. The first plague results in ugly sores. The second plague turns the salt waters to blood and all living creatures in the sea die. The third plague turns fresh waters into blood. The justice of God: the wicked shed innocent blood, now God gives them blood to drink.

Nathaniel Hawthorne made this verse (*Rev.* 16:6) the plot on which he built his story, *The House of the Seven Gables.* Matthew Maule is unjustly sentenced to death by Judge Pyncheon. Before the sentence is carried out, Maule curses Pyncheon, saying, "God will give you blood to drink." And it happens throughout the story, until the injustice is at long last atoned.

The fourth plague brings scorching heat. And sad to say, these disasters do not convert the wicked. As the plagues in Egypt only hardened the Pharaoh's heart, so here the wicked *blasphemed the name of God . . . but they did not repent, or give Him glory (Rev.* 16:9).

The fifth plague brought darkness, pains and sores. And only hardened the wicked the more, for *they did not repent of their works* (16:11).

The sixth plague dried up the Euphrates River making it possible for the fierce kings of the East, the Parthians, to invade pagan Rome.

An intermediate vision intrudes before the seventh plague: three unclean spirits like frogs come out of the mouth of the diabolical trinity, the dragon and the two beasts. Croaking like frogs, they muster the forces of evil against God. But God comes like a thief in the night and destroys them suddenly and completely as were the wicked Canaanites by Deborah and Barak (*Jgs.* 5:1-23) and the marauding Midianites by Gideon (*Jgs.* 7) on the hill of Megiddo *(Armageddon) (Rev.* 16:13-16).

The seventh plague follows as the grand finale. The great city, pagan Rome, is rent by violent earthquakes and pounded by huge hailstones. The punishment of Rome will be commensurate with its iniquity; that is, unprecedented, such as never had been *since the human race began on earth.* In Chapter 17, John will describe these events in greater detail.

The terrible thing in all these visitations of God is that far from curing the wicked, they become worse. There are four kinds of people: 1. **the superficially good**—in times of crisis they become bad, like Judas; 2. **the really good**—in times of crisis they become better as the martyrs in Revelation; 3. **the really bad**—in times of crisis they become worse, as did the wicked when visited with the plagues in Revelation; and 4. **the superficially bad**—in times of crisis, they become good, like the good thief on the cross.

Our Lady told Fr. Gobbi that what happened in John's day is happening now in our own day. *The hour of great tribulation,* she said, *has now descended upon the world, because the angels of the Lord are being sent, with their plagues, to chastise the world* (#412).

Never as today have immorality, impurity and obscenity been so continually propagandized through the press, the television, movies and rock music. Human and Christian dignity is constantly being profaned.

In the name of freedom, all the sins of impurity are being justified and legitimated: homosexuality, adultery, abortion, the use of artificial contraception, sex education leading youth to impurity, pre-marital sex.

Mary said, *God is being continually offended by the sins of the flesh. And so, the Angel of the first plague is passing over the world. . . (inflicting) grave and incurable maladies* (#412).

The first plague is that of malignant tumors and every kind of cancer. Our Lady said many who are good and innocent may be stricken, but their suffering will serve for the salvation of many of the wicked in virtue of the solidarity which unites us all.

The first plague is (also) the new malady of AIDS, which strikes. . . victims of drugs, of vices and of impure sins against nature (#412).

The counterpart to physical AIDS is ecclesiastical AIDS: Apostasy (because of errors being taught), Infidelity (due to a loss of a sense of sin), Disunity (due to dissent) and Sacriligious communions (#340).

To combat these plagues, Our Lady asks that we: *Walk along the road of fasting, mortification and penance.* To those stricken, she says: *Do not despair. I urge you all to look to me, your heavenly Mother, that you may be comforted and assisted.* Turn to your heavenly Mother and offer your pains in reparation.

At the priests retreat in Malvern, Pennsylvania, November 14, 1990, Our Lady repeated the same message. She said:

The hour of the great trial has arrived for your nation, for your Church and for all humanity.
However she called this hour, *the moment of the divine justice and mercy.* Note she is saying that God's justice is now being tempered by His mercy. God wills our elemental disasters, maladies and sufferings, not to destroy us, but to save us; to bring us to our senses: to Himself; just as disasters brought sinners to Himself in John's day. . .*there was a great earthquake, and a tenth of the city fell in ruins. Seven thousand people were killed during the earthquake; the rest were terrified and gave glory to the God of heaven (Rev.* 11:13).

You see, fear from the catastrophe brought many back to God. The fear of the Lord is the beginning of wisdom. God had tried the soft touch in Eden. It did not work. Now He has nothing left to move sinners to repent but fear evoked by disasters, maladies, sufferings. Fear can beget wisdom and can lead to love. *Per crucem ad lucem*—through the cross to the light.

CHAPTER 14

The Judgment of Babylon
(*Revelation* 17)

John now describes in greater detail and in more vivid imagery the sixth and the seventh plagues.

First, he uses the usual introductory vision. Its object is pagan Rome: *I will show you the great harlot who lives near the many waters*—water is the symbol of evil (*Jer.* 51:13). Other pagan kings and their subjects, the inhabitants of the earth, had committed fornication with her; that is, they went along with the cult of emperor worship.

Then John was carried to a deserted place where he *saw a woman seated on a scarlet beast that was covered with blasphemous names, with seven heads and ten horns* (17:3).

The woman is seated on a scarlet beast; for, like the dragon, she perpetrates evil that is both monstrous and murderous. The beast was covered with blasphemous names, for Caesar demanded the worship that belongs to God alone. The beast is pagan Rome, for it is a city seated on seven hills. And the ten horns are the emperors of pagan Rome. Domitian is the tenth Roman emperor from Tiberius. The woman was seated on the scarlet beast "in a deserted place," for evil is sterile and spawns a wasteland.

Yet the woman has a certain attraction—the attraction of a prostitute, clad in royal purple and scarlet and bedecked with gold, precious stones and pearls. *She held in her hand a gold cup,* not filled with wine, but *with abominable and* sordid deeds: idolatry and murder (*Rev.* 17:4). *The woman was drunk on the blood of the holy ones and on the blood of the witnesses of Jesus* (*Rev.* 17:6).

On her forehead was written a name, as required of prostitutes by Roman law. The name was *Babylon the great, the mother of harlots and of the abominations of the earth* (*Rev.* 17:5).

The Jews in the Old Testament looked upon Babylon as the embodiment of all evil. Babylon was rooted in evil, for the tower of Babel was the symbol of human arrogance, pride and rebellion against God. In 586 B.C., Babylon destroyed Jerusalem and enslaved her children, transporting them into exile in Babylon.

The new Babylon is the pagan Rome of the Caesars—*the beast with seven heads and ten horns.* She is called "the great," because she outstripped by far the evils of Babylon of old and all the other "babylons" (symbol of everything evil): Tyre and Nineveh and Samaria.

The angel explains the meaning of the vision to John. *The seven heads represent seven hills upon which the woman sits. They also represent seven kings: five have already fallen, one still lives and the last has not yet come, and when he comes he must remain only for a short while. The beast that existed once, but exists no longer is an eighth king, but really belongs to the seven and is headed for destruction* (*Rev.* 17:9-11).

The five kings already fallen were probably Augustus, Tiberias, Caligula, Claudius, and Nero. One still lives, namely, Vespasian—John probably had this vision during Vespasian's reign (69-79 A.D.), when there was a cessation in persecution. "The last who has not yet come" was Titus, the son of Vespasian. Titus destroyed Jerusalem and was emperor for only a short time (79-81 A.D.). The eighth king is Domitian (81-96), thought to be another Nero. Thus John says he really belongs to the seven. Yet he too, like Nero, is headed for destruction. Actually, Domitian was assassinated on September 18 in the year 96 A.D.

The ten horns of the beast represent pagan rulers, who think like the beast regarding idolatry and emperor worship, and therefore who share the authority of the beast, but only for a short while—"one hour." They too will persecute the Church, but in vain—God's chosen and faithful ones and the Lamb will conquer them, for He is Lord of lords and King of kings.

Then, in God's own good time, even these pagan kings will unwittingly fulfill God's purpose against pagan Rome. They will hate her and eventually leave her desolate and naked.

CHAPTER 15

The Fall of Babylon
The Seven Sights
(*Revelation* 18-20)

Chapter 18 and 19:
   The first sight (*Rev.* 18:1-8). *After this, I saw another angel coming down from heaven. . .and he cried out in a mighty voice: 'Fallen, fallen is Babylon the great.'* Then he gives the reason for her fall: immorality and the shedding of innocent blood.

   Then John heard another voice warning the faithful to leave pagan Rome before its fall, lest they be corrupted by her sins or be caught up in her destruction.

   The second sight (*Rev.* 18:9-10). The kings of the earth, the home merchants and the seafaring merchants weep for the fall of pagan Rome, but only for economic reasons: the loss of a lucrative market. The holy ones, on the contrary, rejoice at her fall.

   The third sight (*Rev.* 18:21-24). A mighty angel picked up a huge millstone and threw it into the sea and said in effect, "Thus shall pagan Rome be destroyed—completely. It shall vanish, like a millstone hurled into the sea. There will be no melody, no song, no joy—only stark silence."

   The fourth sight (*Rev.* 19:1-10). In contrast, the saints in Heaven will break out into ecstatic joy over pagan Rome's fall, singing "Alleluia!" The twenty-four elders and the four living creatures will concur and join the rejoicing, saying, "Amen. Alleluia."

A voice from the throne invites all the servants of God to praise the Lord. The response is a Victory song, sounding like rushing water or the peals of thunder.

Handel had this chapter in mind when he composed his immortal Oratorio *"The Messiah"*—which he did in twenty-four days (from August 24 to September 14, 1741). The Oratorio opened in Dublin, and Handel used the proceeds from the performance to free 142 debtors from prison. He had set the pattern: during his lifetime every performance of the Messiah was for charitable purposes. I am sure, the Messiah was well-pleased.

The thunderous, stirring "Hallelujah Chorus" seems inspired. Handel said he endeavored to picture to himself what the great gladness of the glorified must be. "Hallelujah! For the Lord God omnipotent reigneth. The kingdom of this world is become the kingdom of our Lord, and of His Christ; and He shall reign forever and ever. King of kings and Lord of lords. Hallelujah!"

The cause for this musical outburst was that the reign of God had been established by conquest and the wedding day of the Lamb to His bride, the Church, has come.

John was so swept away with emotion that he actually knelt down to worship the angel, a widespread tendency in Asia Minor at the time. But the angel rebuked him severely saying, *Worship God!*

The fifth sight (*Rev.* 19:11-21). *Then I saw the heavens opened* and Christ, the Word of God, appeared as a warrior, conqueror, invincible King—Lord of lords. Faithful to His followers and true to His word, He fights for justice. His eyes blaze like fiery flame in anger against the enemies of God. His cloak has been dipped in the blood of Calvary. Behind Him ride the armies of Heaven. He pronounces judgment:

out of his mouth came a sharp sword to strike the nations. And He crushes them, like grapes in a winepress.

Victory is written in flaming letters across the book of Revelation. If more Christians knew this book, they would never succumb to a defeatist attitude in the face of the world's evils. It is too bad, also, that artists do not go more often to Revelation for their portraits of Christ. In the National Shrine of the Immaculate Conception in Washington, D.C., the artist John De Rosen has caught something of the Christ of Revelation in his mosaic behind the main altar—the "Christ in Majesty." In the arch above this mosaic is inscribed the words: "Christ Conquers, Christ Reigns, Christ Rules, Eternal Victor, Eternal King, Eternal Master, His Power Is an Everlasting Power, That Shall Not be Taken Away."

Next, John saw an angel standing on the sun, calling to the birds flying high in the sky to eat the enemies of God. The beast and the false prophet (the satellite kings of Rome) were hurled down alive into the fiery pool burning with sulphur. The rest—*those who had accepted the mark of the beast*—were killed by the sword and given as food to the vultures.

Chapter 20
The sixth sight (*Rev.* 20:1-10). *Then I saw an angel come down from heaven, holding in his hand the key to the abyss and a heavy chain. . . He seized the dragon and tied him up for a 1000 years.*

A thousand years simply signifies the life of the Church on earth. The life of the Church on earth has two sides: a negative and a positive one.

Negatively, the Church on earth is the target of suffering, temptation, persecution. John refers to this side of the Church by the numbers three and one half years (the time of the terrible persecution of the Jews by Antiochus, June 168 to Dec. 165 B.C.) or 42 months or 1260 days.

Positively, the Church on earth is engaged in deadly conflict with a devil whose powers have been limited mightily by the death and resurrection of Christ. Christ has entered the strong man's house, the devil, and plundered it (*Mt.*12:29). As a result, *the one begotten by God he protects, and the evil one cannot touch him* (*1 Jn.* 5:18; *Col.* 2:15). When John refers to this aspect of the Church, he uses the number one thousand. (Seven plus the three of the Trinity equals ten; ten tripled equals one thousand, the symbol of the Church triumphant on earth). Christ's death and resurrection has chained the devil. St. Augustine said, "Who gets bit by a chained dog has only himself to blame."

William Blatty's book *The Exorcist* opens in Mesopotamia. A Jesuit archaelogist has finished exploring there. One of the things he found buried in the dig was a green stone head of the demon Pazuzu. The implication was that before the Church of Christ, devil worship was rampant in the ancient world. Satan had conquered.

Then the scene shifts from the East to the West, to Washington, D.C. A girl, Regan, is possessed by the devil. In this instance, the devil is not worshipped, but exorcised—driven out of Regan by the Church.

In the ancient world, Satan was in control. But since the coming of Christ and His Church, he is no longer in control: he is exorcised, driven out; his power is chained! *I have observed Satan,* Jesus said (in ecstasy after the seventy-two returned from their first mission), *fall like lightning from the sky. Behold, I have given you power to tread upon serpents and scorpions and upon the full force of the enemy and nothing will harm you.* (*Lk.* 10:18-19). Jesus was announcing that the dominion of Satan over the human race was now at an end—the thousand years had begun.

During this thousand years, John distinguishes two classes of people: those who come to life through baptism (the first resurrection), and those who do not (the first death). At the general resurrection, at the end of the thousand years, those who had enjoyed the first resurrection will not taste the second death. Whereas those who had not will suffer the second death: eternal damnation.

After the thousand years, Satan will be released for a short time—for the final judgment. In his pride Satan cannot see that he is defeated, that it's all over for him. For he still, at that late hour, will try to seduce the pagan nations—Gog and Magog—to battle against the holy ones of God. Of course, there is no fight, for Satan has already been conquered on Calvary. All that remains is judgment: *Fire came down from heaven and consumed them* (20:9). Then the devil and all his cohorts were thrown into the pool of fire and sulphur to be tormented day and night forever and ever.

The seventh sight (*Rev.*20:11-15). At last we reach the final judgment. All the dead of the earth stand before the One sitting on a large white throne. The book of life is opened and the dead are judged according to their deeds. Those whose names are not found written in the book of life are thrown into the pool of fire (the second death).

Some heterdox theologians think an everlasting Hell is too cruel for God. They offer two solutions. Some say there will be a general amnesty at the end. Others, like the Jehovah Witnesses, say that there will be an annihilation of the devils and the damned. Final pardon or mercy-killing for the damned.

Someone asked, "Why doesn't God, if He is so merciful, forgive the devil?" The answer is the devil never asked him. Hell is eternal not because God wills it, but because the damned will it.

The devil and the damned are in Hell, because they want to be there. They are not kicking and screaming to get out. Were someone, as an act of charity, to open the door of Hell so that the damned could escape to Heaven, he would be pelted with all manner of unmentionable refuse by spitting and cursing beings within. Sooner or later someone would snarl, "Close the blasted door!" (Paine, *idem* pp. 12 & 81f).

CHAPTER 16

The New Creation
(*Revelation* 21-22:5)

Chapter 21

John has described what happens to the devil and those whose names are not written in the book of life. They go to eternal torments. Now he describes the reward of those whose names *are* written in the book of life. They enter into eternal joy. *Come, you who are blessed by my Father. Inherit the kingdom prepared for you from the foundation of the world* (*Matt.* 25:34).

This Kingdom will be "a new Heaven and a new earth," because the faithful will be there in it and there will be no more danger of defection, no more death or mourning, wailing or pain—for "the sea is no more." The old order has passed away.

But until this comes to pass, Our Lady has asked us (through Fr. Gobbi), to pray to the Holy Spirit to give us *a new Heavens and a new earth here and now, where the Most Holy Trinity will be loved and glorified; where the wounds of egoism and of hatred, of impurity and injustice, may be entirely healed* (#265). Thus we pray, "Send forth thy Spirit and they shall be created; and Thou shalt renew the face of the earth."

The centerpiece of this new creation is a new Jerusalem, *coming down out of Heaven from God, prepared as a bride adorned for her husband* (*Rev.* 21:2). This new Jerusalem is the triumph of the Church.

88

Then the One who sat on the throne, God Himself, states He will make all things new; that the Alpha and the Omega will give the spring of life-giving water to the victor, but the burning pool of fire and sulphur to the cowards and traitors (*Rev.* 21:5).

Now John goes on to describe the new Jerusalem, the Lamb's bride, the Church triumphant. It was radiant, like a sparkling jewel; a city of pure gold, clear as glass. It was secure, with massive walls of jasper, 200 feet high. The walls had twelve gates: three in each wall. Each gate was made from a single pearl. The walls rested on twelve courses of stone—for the city included saints from the Old and New Testament.

The foundations of the city walls were decorated with twelve precious stones: jasper, sapphire, chalcedony, emerald, sardonyx, carnelian, chrysolite, beryl, topaz, chrysoprase, jacinth, amethyst. These twelve stones are the symbols of the signs of the Zodiac, but in reverse order. The ancients believed that in following the Zodiac, they were in tune with the heavens. By reversing the order, can we not say that it is the Church, the people of God, who are in tune with all creation? The city was perfectly square, for it was a city where justice prevailed; a city "fair and square." It was cube-shaped, like the Holy of Holies, for it too templed God. Its proportions were gigantic: 1500 miles long, or 2,250,000 square miles. In other words, there would be room here for everybody (*Rev.* 21:9-21).

To the ancient Greeks, the city of the gods was on Mt. Olympus. The sun, moon and stars, lit the city. The Milky Way was the main street. It too had twelve gates, through which the stars went in and out. Connected with the city were the signs of the Zodiac, that part of the heavens through which the sun passes.

The city of God, unlike Jerusalem, had no temple, for the Lord God almighty and the Lamb were its temple.

Nor like the city of the Grecian gods on Mt. Olympus, the city of God *had no need of sun or moon to shine on it, for the glory of God gave it light and its lamp was the Lamb* (*Rev.* 21:23). Only those whose names are written in the Lamb's book of life will enter this city.

Down through the main street of this city flows a river of life-giving water. On either side of the river grew the tree of life. The Bible began with paradise; it ends with paradise. In Eden four rivers flowed; here only one river of life-giving water flows—water from the side of Christ: life-giving grace. In Eden there was only one tree of life; here there are two, producing fruit twelves times a year, once each month. The fruits are the saints, so diverse. They see God face to face in this city that knows no night and that endures forever. The entire scene is reminiscent of man in his innocence in the garden of Eden (*Rev.* 22:1-5).

But until all this comes to pass, Our Lady continues to ask us to work here and now for the new Jerusalem come down from Heaven, as a bride adorned for her husband. We are to help renew the dwelling place of God among mankind. Through the Holy Spirit, we must pray for a Church renewed by the Spirit, for a Church faithful to the gospel, for a Church humble, chaste and merciful.

The new heavens and the new earth will be a time of grace: a time when the power of God's grace and glory will become .manifest more and more in His people.

The Church will be a new Jerusalem, the holy City, without spot or blemish or wrinkle. When Pope John XXIII convoked the Vatican Council, he stated in his opening address that the sole purpose of the Council was not to condemn any errors, but to reform the Church, to turn in on the Church herself, examine her own conscience, so to speak, and to reform what needs to be renewed so that the Pope could hold up the bride of Christ, the Church, to all the world in its unblemished glory, and say to our separated brothers and sisters, "This is the Bride of Christ. Return home so that there will be one fold, one faith, one Shepherd."

Thus the aims of the Council were threefold: the three R's—Reform, leading to Renewal, leading to Reunion. When this happens, God will dwell among His people and there will be joy, like that of a bride on her wedding day.

We can help achieve this by living vigorously the Communion of Saints. The saints in Heaven by their powerful assistance and intercession help us overcome the dangers, obstacles, and difficulties strewn across the road we must travel. We ought to pray with the souls in purgatory; this communion of prayer shortens their stay there and gives us security and courage to face the difficulties presented by the world and to do God's will.

If we live this stupendous reality of the communion of saints, it will unite us, help us and pledge us to fight for the full triumph of Christ, and bring His glorious reign here on earth in our own lifetime.

The Epilogue (*Rev.* 22:6-21) is a series of warnings and exhortations tied in with the themes and expressions of the Prologue.

The angel of the vision testifies that all that John has been told is true. When John once again falls to his knees to worship the angel, the angel, a second time, remonstrates, saying, *Worship God.*

Three times God says, *I am coming soon.* God had said this four times in the letters to the churches; thus making seven times in all. *I am coming soon* to reward each according to his works: the wicked with damnation; the holy ones with eternal joys.

Blessed are they who wash their robes by good deeds, they will have a right to the tree of life and enter the city through its gates.

John warns us that this is the testimony of Jesus, the root of David. Therefore add nothing to it, nor subtract anything from it. The One Who gives this testimony says, *Yes, I am coming soon.*

The Spirit and His bride, the Church, just can't wait and they say, "Come."

So ought we, all of us who thirst for the life-giving water say, *Marana, tha—Lord Jesus, come!* Come in power and majesty. Come in judgment. Take over this world. We are tired of living in a world where you are not Lord, where those who follow you are persecuted. Let your kingdom come on earth as it is in Heaven. Come and conquer evil. Come and reign. Come and rule.

Jesus answers, *Yes, I am coming soon.*

The grand conclusion, therefore, for all of us is to live in patient endurance, the victory is sure.

May "the grace of the Lord Jesus be with all." Amen.

About the Author

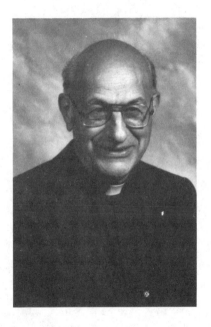

Reverend Albert J.M. Shamon was ordained for the Diocese of Rochester in 1940. He has served as a pastor, teacher, columnist, author and radio broadcaster. In 1990 he celebrated his 50th anniversary in the priesthood, and concelebrated Mass with John Paul II at the Pope's private chapel in Rome. Currently, Father Shamon is administrator of St. Isaac Jogues Parish in Fleming, N.Y., and resides in Auburn, New York.

Books
By Rev. Albert J. M. Shamon

Our Lady Teaches About Prayer at Medjugorje

Our Lady Says: Let Holy Mass be Your Life

Our Lady Says: Monthly Confession —
Remedy for the West

Our Lady Teaches About Sacramentals
and Blessed Objects

Our Lady Says: Pray the Creed

Three Steps to Sanctity

The Power of the Rosary

Our Lady Says: Love People

The Ten Commandments of God

Behind the Mass

Apocalypse - A Book For Our Times

Firepower Through Confirmation

Genesis: The Book of Origins

Exodus: Road to Freedom

A Graphic Life of Jesus the Christ

For additional information, contact **THE RIEHLE
FOUNDATION**, distributor of Catholic Books.

Please write to: **THE RIEHLE FOUNDATION
P.O. Box 7
Milford Oh 45150-0007
513-576-0032**

THE
RIEHLE
FOUNDATION

ıehle Foundation is a non-profit, tax-exempt,
ɔ organization that exists to produce and/or dis-
Catholic material to individuals and bookstores.

ıe Foundation is dedicated to the Mother of God and
role in the salvation of mankind. We believe that this
ıe has not diminished in our time but, on the contrary, has
ɔecome all the more apparent in this the era of Mary as
recognized by Pope John Paul II.

Since its inception in 1976, the Foundation has
distributed books, films, rosaries, bibles, etc. to individuals,
parishes, organizations, and foreign countries all over the
world. Additionally, the Foundation sends materials to
prison chaplains, hospitals, and outreach ministries.

Your prayers and donations to The Riehle Foundation
for the materials distributed are deeply appreciated.

IN THE SERVICE OF JESUS AND MARY
All for the honor and glory of God!

The Riehle Foundation
P.O. Box 7
Milford, OH 45150-0007 USA
513-576-0032
www.riehlefoundation.com